WHAT HAPPENS TO
GOOD PEOPLE
WHEN BAD THINGS
HAPPEN

Other books by Robert A. Schuller

Power to Grow Beyond Yourself

Strength for the Fragile Spirit

*Just Because You're on a Roll . . .
Doesn't Mean You're Going Downhill*

*Dump Your Hang-Ups without
Dumping Them on Others*

WHAT HAPPENS TO GOOD PEOPLE WHEN BAD THINGS HAPPEN

Robert A. Schuller

Fleming H. Revell
A Division of Baker Book House Co
Grand Rapids, Michigan 49516

© 1995 by Robert A. Schuller

Published by Fleming H. Revell
a division of Baker Book House Company
P.O. Box 6287, Grand Rapids, MI 49516-6287

Printed in the United States of America

Library of Congress Cataloging-in-Publication Data

Schuller, Robert A.
  What happens to good people when bad things happen / Robert A. Schuller.
     p.   cm.
  ISBN 0-8007-1712-0
    1. Suffering—Religious aspects—Christianity. 2. Consolation. I. Title.
BV4909.S38   1995
248.8'6—dc20   95-8642

Contents

1

When Terrible Things Happen to Terrific People

I couldn't believe it when the phone call came.

Ed Loynes was in a coma and not expected to live.

How could it be possible? He was the picture of health. Except, that is, for that problem with his knee. But that was nothing new. The knee had been bothering him for years. It was one of those annoying aches that seem to come along with age.

Although he was fifty-eight years of age, Alan seemed anything but old. He had always kept himself in shape and looked to be five to ten years younger than he really was. He was active, vibrant, and friendly—a good husband and father. Everyone who knew him felt the same about him. He was a good man.

Then the phone call came and his daughter told me, gasping through her tears, what had happened.

It seems that a couple of days before, Ed had decided to go have some cartilage and scar tissue removed from his knee. It was no big deal. It was outpatient surgery, in fact, and he had driven himself home from the hospital.

But then he had started feeling weak. He developed a high fever. An infection was sweeping through his body, and by the time he was sick enough to be taken back to the hospital, the doctors didn't know if there was anything they could do to save him.

For two days Ed lay in a coma.

The third day was his fifty-ninth birthday.

The fourth day he died without ever having regained consciousness.

I understood how his wife felt when she came to me before his funeral and asked, Why did this happen?

I didn't blame his children when they said, We just don't understand how God could have allowed this to happen. He was such a good man.

Those heartfelt questions were merely the echoes of the same desperate voices I've heard dozens of times before. This is a question that has haunted men and women for centuries: Why do bad things happen to good people? Why, indeed. Why is a beautiful teenage girl who's headed to college on an academic scholarship killed in a car accident the week after her graduation from high school? Why is a young man left paralyzed after he dives into a swimming pool and hits his head on the bottom? Why does a young mother of small children come down with life-threatening cancer? Why does a man who has worked hard all of his life suddenly have his entire savings wiped out?

These are just some of the situations I have had to confront in my work as a minister.

And then there are the other situations that may be less dramatic but are just as troubling and painful to those passing through them. There are the aches and pains of daily life that can become almost too much to bear.

Why is this the way things are? Certainly, you know what I'm talking about:

if you are dealing with grief.

if you have lost a friend to death or disability.

if you have failed in business, family matters, friendships, or morals.

if you are overcome with inferiority thoughts or negative thinking.

if you are dealing with the pain of a broken marriage or relationship.

if all of your hard work and efforts have gone for nothing.

if you find yourself somewhere you never wanted to be.

if you feel life pushing you down.

if you feel like a failure as a parent or a spouse.

if it seems that life for you has been one long losing streak.

if it's a struggle to get out of bed in the morning because you don't want to face another day.

if you wonder when everything went wrong and where all the "good days" went.

If you see yourself in any of these situations, take heart! I'm writing to tell you that there is a ray of hope. More than a ray, in fact. A *floodlight* of hope is shining throughout the darkness of the universe.

You see, God loves you. He has not forsaken you. He has not forgotten you. He cares deeply for you—so much, in fact, that he is pouring out his blessings upon you.

You may be saying, Well, I sure don't *feel* blessed.

I understand that.

But it doesn't change the fact that God *is* blessing you, even now, in the midst of your pain. I want to help you discover those blessings that will guide you safely through the present darkness.

It amazes me that some people like to point fingers at those who are going through a tough time. They'll tell you, Well, you must be doing something wrong, or these things wouldn't happen to you.

But God's book, the Bible, tells us over and over again that this is simply not true.

The entire Book of Job, for instance, was written to dispel the false notion that bad things only happen to bad people.

Turn to the ninth chapter of the Book of John and you'll find Jesus dealing with the same subject. It seems that he and his apostles were walking down a street in Jerusalem when they came across a man who had been blind from birth.

The apostles asked Jesus, "Who sinned, this man, or his parents?" As far as they were concerned, those were the only options available. The man was blind. Therefore, there must be wrong behavior somewhere in his life.

Jesus quickly set them straight. The man wasn't blind because of sin—either his own sin or that of his parents. Instead, Jesus said, the man was blind "that the glory of God might be revealed." And then he healed the man's blindness.

When you are suffering or in pain—whether your pain is physical, emotional, or spiritual—that's a time when the glory of God can be revealed to you in new and exciting ways. It's a time when you can lean on God and find out how much he really cares. It is a time when you can grow in faith and trust and when God's strength can be seen more clearly in your weakness.

The Bible tells us that the rain falls on the just and the unjust alike (Matt. 5:45). And it's true.

If you walk long enough you're bound to stub your toe some time or other. If you ride your bike long enough, you'll probably fall off at least once. No matter what you do in life, there are bound to be some negative consequences occasionally. You will experience some bad times, some hard knocks, some tough challenges. All those things are part of living.

Ed died at the relatively early age of fifty-nine.

But how old would be old enough? Has a man lived a full life if he dies at sixty-nine? Or seventy-nine? Or one hundred-nine? How old is old enough?

The simple fact is that every day we live is another day that God has given to us. It's another gift from his hand—and how much happier we would all be if that's how we viewed it.

The prophet Isaiah said it this way: "All men are like grass, and all their glory is like the flowers of the field. The grass withers, and the flowers fall, because the breath of the Lord blows on them" (40:6–7).

And yet the Bible also tells us that "our present sufferings are not worth comparing with the glory that will be revealed in us" (Rom. 8:18). And "we know that in all things God works for the good of those who love him" (Rom. 8:28).

That is the Word of God. It stands forever. If you look at the course of history, from the beginning of time until the end of time, God is always there. He has always been and always will be.

Suffering may last for a moment, or even a lifetime—but the blessings of God will last for all eternity. What's more, I am convinced that God wants to bless you right now!

I don't know your heart, but God does. And the Bible tells us that he "delights" in giving us the desires of our hearts. But I am convinced that he also expects us to work with him.

One of the reasons I'm writing this book is to help you see some of the ways you can "work" with him, so you can get into position to receive the best he has to offer—the things he really wants to give you.

I'm also writing this book to help you see the blessings that God has already given you. My desire is that when we are finished with our time together, you will feel closer to God than you have ever felt before. I want you to feel more secure in his love than you've ever felt before. I want you to have the understanding that God is really in charge of this universe, and that he can put all of the seemingly discordant pieces of your life together into a cohesive and beautiful whole. He will bring things together in just the right way for you, the way various notes of music come together to form a symphony. Trust him, honor him, and it *will* happen.

In the chapters ahead, some of the things I want to talk about are:

- What the Bible means when it says that God gives his "eternal blessings to good people."
- How God is blessing you, even when life hurts.
- How you can feel the peace of God.
- How you can feel the comfort of God's forgiveness.
- How you can obtain blessing, even in the midst of your pain, by reaching out to others.
- How you can obtain refuge from the storms of life.
- How God wants you to feel the blessing of the joy of his presence.
- How you can be blessed through God's instruction.
- How God is blessing you by allowing you to use his name.
- Why you can face the future with total confidence.

I'm excited about the journey we're about to take, and I hope you are, too.

Are you ready to start? Let's go!

2

Ouch, That Hurts!
Thank You, Lord!

Sometimes the blessings of God come in the most unexpected ways.

For Margaret, his blessings came in the form of an irritating, untimely and, if the truth be told, downright obnoxious phone call—a phone call that saved her life.

At the time, she thought it was merely going to make her late for choir practice—and that was something she definitely didn't want to happen because she was due to sing a solo on Sunday morning. And not just *any* solo. This was a difficult number, one that required lots of practice with the rest of the choir.

Margaret had already grabbed her purse and coat and was halfway out the door when her phone rang on that winter's evening. For a moment, she considered ignoring it—especially when she glanced at her watch and realized that she'd be right on time if she left *now!* But, like most of the rest of us, a ring-ing telephone was something Margaret found impossible to ignore. What if it was something urgent?

It wasn't.

"Congratulations," rang out the voice on the other end of the line. "I'm calling to tell you that you've won one of three special prizes!"

"I'm sorry, but I—"

"You've won either a brand new television set, a Las Vegas vacation, or—"

"I really don't have time—"

"All you have to do to claim your prizes is to come for a visit."

Some people might have said something rude and slammed down the phone. But as annoyed as Margaret was, she thought, *Well, this person is only trying to do her job. I can't blame her.*

It took at least two or three minutes for her politely to inform the caller that she wasn't interested in collecting her prizes, that she was late for something important and she had to go. Then she ran out to her car, feeling badly that she was going to keep the others waiting.

She was still about a block away from her church when it happened. Suddenly, the sky was filled with the brightest light she had ever seen. It was dark—and then it was bright as day. A couple of seconds after the light reached her eyes, her eardrums were blasted by a deafening roar.

Margaret slammed her foot on the brake, bringing her car to a squealing, swerving stop in the middle of the street. Her hands were shaking and her heart was pounding so loud she could hear it. *What was that?* she thought. *A bomb?*

No doubt, something up there had exploded, and now flames were shooting hundreds of feet into the night sky. From all over the neighborhood, people were running in the direction of the flames.

"What was that?" someone yelled.

"The church," came the reply. "It must have been a bomb."

Margaret got out of her car, leaving it sitting in the middle of the street, and slowly walked in the direction of the church. Indeed, the entire structure was engulfed in flames. (She found out later that it wasn't a bomb, but rather a leaking gas connection.)

As she stood looking at the conflagration, she remembered the phone call. Without that annoying interruption, she undoubtedly would have been inside that church, which meant, in turn, that she would have been dead.

Strangely enough, Margaret wasn't the only choir member who was late to the practice that night. Every single person in the choir had experienced some sort of last-minute interruption. As they gathered in front of the church, holding hands and thanking God, the choir members knew that if things had gone as they normally would have on a regular night, every one of them would have been killed.

The Blessings Are Real

It is not always easy to see the blessings of God as they unfold. Sometimes, they even seem to come in the form of an annoyance—as Margaret's did—or they may even come in the middle of a time of sorrow or trouble. One thing I can assure you, though, is that God *is* blessing you and he is doing it right now.

In fact, not only is he blessing you now, but he wants to bless you more. He wants you to open up your heart and your soul and receive all the good things he has to give you.

I don't know who you are, but I do know that whoever you are, whatever you do, wherever you live, you *need* the blessings of God in your life!

Are you going through a tough time? Do you sometimes find yourself wondering what happened—how you got to this terrible point in your life? Perhaps you find yourself looking back on "the good old days" that were so filled with promise and hope and wondering exactly where it was that you took the wrong turn?

I don't know what's going on in your life right now. Maybe financial problems are crowding in on you to the point where it's difficult to breathe. Perhaps you've lost someone you loved. Maybe you're sick and in continuous pain. Or maybe you're just tired of fighting your way upstream against a raging current. You're exhausted and feel like giving up and letting life carry you wherever it will.

I don't know how hurt you feel, how frustrated you are, or how the actions of others have damaged you. But I do know one thing: God is there. And he *is* blessing you, right in the middle of whatever it is you're going through.

Think about this for a moment: Have you ever gone through a time in your life that you thought was really tough but when you look back on it, it seems like it really wasn't so bad? Maybe it was even a lot of fun.

For example, it might be the time when you were first married, when you and your spouse were just starting out in life. You may not have had much money. You may have lived in an apartment that was so small you had to go outside to turn around. You may have had things so tight financially that you subsisted for weeks on nothing more than soup and bread. But looking back on it, you can see that even though the particulars of the moment may not have been pleasant, it was a pretty good time after all. It was a time when a lot of good things were going on in your life—when you and your spouse were really getting to know each other, and when the hard times were made palatable by the fact that you had each other to lean on.

When you were going through it, you may have thought that the blessings of God might as well have been millions of light years away. But now you can see that through it all, God was there, and that somehow he managed to weave a beautiful tapestry out of the individual threads of your suffering.

> *Whatever*
> *is happening in your life,*
> *God is there,*
> *and he is blessing you now!*

In the same way, the blessings of God are being poured on you right now in many ways. All you have to do is open your eyes to see them and then open your arms to accept them.

Whatever is happening in your life, God is there, and he is blessing you now!

Let me ask you a question. What do you say when somebody sneezes? You probably say, God bless you.

What do you say when you're not going to see someone for a while and you want to wish them well? Again, your most likely comment is, God bless you.

That's what *I* say (and I'm admitting this because I don't want you to think I'm picking on you), but I think we've got things all mixed up when we say God bless you. Why? Because that is saying, in effect, I hope God will bless you in the future.

What we ought to be saying is, God *is* blessing you! We need to have an understanding that his blessings are continuous and that he is *always* with us.

Sometimes I hear people pray, and they beg God to be with them: Oh, Lord, please be with me and bless me as I leave on this business trip. The implication of a prayer like this is that you've got to beg God to be with you or otherwise he won't.

I am not saying that a prayer that asks for God's blessings and protection is wrong—not at all. What I am saying is that we need to have a better understanding of God's presence and blessing in our lives. Instead of saying, Lord, please be with me and bless me, it would be far better to say, Lord, thank you for being with me. Thank you for blessing me. A prayer like this shows a proper understanding of the ways God is working in the lives of his people.

You can be certain that when you don't have the strength to stand, God will carry you. When you don't know where to go, he will lead you. When you don't know what to say, he will speak through you. He will touch you wherever you are. He *is* blessing you and not in some abstract way that doesn't really mean anything.

I believe that God is blessing each of us in very real, very tangible ways and I am writing this book to help you discover and uncover those blessings. Once you have a better understanding of the ways in which God is blessing you and the ways in which he wants to bless you, then you can do a better job of appropriating those blessings and putting them to work in your life.

From Darkness to Light

If you are sorrowful, God is blessing you in the midst of your sorrow. If you are lonely, God is bending down to bless you in the middle of your loneliness. If you are ill, God is blessing you in the midst of your illness. If you are grieving or coping with loss in some other way, God is blessing you in the midst of that.

There can be no greater comfort than knowing that God loves you, is present with you and is blessing you *all* the time—and he is.

It used to be fairly easy for most of us who live in sunny Southern California to believe and understand that God was blessing us. After all, we had one warm sunny day after another, followed by exhilaratingly cool nights that made it exciting just to be alive. We had snow-capped mountains, beautiful beaches, and rugged deserts. In other words, we seemed to be surrounded by a playground God had designed just for those of us who were fortunate enough to call California home.

My church, Rancho Capistrano Community Church, is in the beautiful coastal community of San Juan Capistrano. We are not very far from the resort city of Laguna Beach. You may remember what happened in Laguna Beach last winter. Fire!

It started in the hills outside of town and roared straight for the city's most luxurious residential areas. By the time firefighters arrived on the scene, the city was all but surrounded by a wall of flame that soared to heights of nearly one hundred feet. There was no way to contain the monstrous blaze, which hungrily devoured everything in its path. One after another, million dollar homes were turned into burnt matchsticks. Thousands of acres of prime California real estate were also consumed and left looking like something that belonged on the moon—or Mars.

Meanwhile, other fires were blazing out of control in other areas of California. Hundreds of homes were destroyed in Malibu, Thousand Oaks, and Altadena. For a while, it seemed that all of California was on fire. Everywhere you looked, the sky was dark with smoke. Ashes swirled out of the sky all day and night, piling up on sidewalks and streets miles away from the blazes themselves. Flames were lashing out at the "Golden State" in all directions.

While we went through many anxious hours in San Juan Capistrano, we were grateful that a shift in the direction of the wind, and a change for the better in the weather, enabled the firefighters to bring one of those fires—the Ortega blaze—under control before it became a serious threat to our community. At the same time, our relief at being spared was coupled with the sorrow and sympathy we felt for those who had been devastated by the fires. There were few deaths, but there were hundreds of families who lost their homes along with all of their possessions. Some escaped with nothing more than the clothes on their backs.

During those terrible days, Californians learned an awful lot about adversity. But that wasn't the end of it. Less than two months later, a 6.8 earthquake rocked the Los Angeles area, toppling apartment buildings, collapsing freeways, and killing dozens of people. The quake destroyed millions of dollars worth of property and left hundreds of people injured, in addition to the thousands of people who were permanently traumatized by the experience.

But you know what? God was blessing those of us who lived in California during those times of disaster. I don't mean that he was blessing those of us who managed to escape the worst of the fire and the quake. I mean that he was blessing those who faced the worst and were forced to flee their houses with nothing more than the clothes they were wearing. I mean that he was blessing those who were caught up in the terror of that 6.8 earthquake.

For one thing, in the days immediately following the earthquake our area newspapers had many stories of self-sacrificing heroism—people who put their own lives on the line in order to rescue and help their friends and neighbors who had been caught in the middle of the disaster. It's often true that a tragedy brings out the very best in people.

I also read of at least one instance where a shaky marriage was put back together by the shaking of the earth. That's because there's nothing like an earthquake to make you think about what is and is not important. Earthquakes have a way of showing trivialities for what they are. When you're faced with the prospect of losing someone you love, all of a sudden possessions aren't so important to you anymore.

But most of all, the earthquake blessed us by bringing home the knowledge that this earth and everything on it is temporary, whereas God's love and power are eternal.

How good to know that even though heaven and earth will pass away, the Word of God will last forever! (Matt. 24:35).

In fact, there is a sense in which the very worst of times can be the best of times. After all, it is in darkness that the light of God's love shines its brightest. It is in the midst of pain that his healing love can be felt most keenly. And it is in the weakness of utter defeat that we can be filled up with his strength.

One of the things that tends to happen when people are passing through a time of difficulty is that they lose sight of God's presence in their lives. They are able to look back and see the ways God has blessed them in the past. They may even be able to look toward the future with hope that God will return his blessings to them. But they look around right now and wonder why God has deserted them. In the present, they feel nothing but deep, dark despair, and when they try to pray about it, their prayers seem to fall to the floor with a thud instead of rising up to heaven. They cannot see the blessings of God shining through their personal darkness.

And yet it has always been God's desire to bless his people. If you go back to Genesis, the first book of the Bible, and read the account of the creation, you will find that God is continually interested in blessing his people. When he created the world, when he created man and woman and put them into this world, he wanted them to be blessed. The New Testament teaches the same thing. When Jesus preached his very first sermon, he began with the words, "Blessed are . . ." He then went on to repeat those two words eight more times during the next few minutes! Clearly, the blessings were real to Christ (see Matt. 5:1–11).

Look and See

Some people don't think God is concerned with the minute details of life. They believe that God set the universe in motion, as if he were winding some giant watch spring, and then he went off and left man to fend for himself. I am convinced that these people couldn't possibly be farther from the truth. If they would look around them—*really* look around them—they would see God's loving care built into nature in so many ways that it would amaze them. (And once they have come to see the loving designs God has built into nature, that should open their eyes to the blessings he provides on a personal and private level as well.)

For example, consider the placement of the planet earth. If we were any farther away from the sun, the atmosphere of the planet would be much too cold to sustain life; any closer and we would all be walking around on hot coals all the time. If gravity were any weaker, the planet earth would go careening out into deepest space; any stronger, and we would be pulled rapidly toward fiery destruction in the center of the sun.

And there's more. The earth is just the right size. If our planet were substantially smaller, gravity would be so weak we would all go floating off into the wild blue yonder; substantially bigger, and the increased gravity would cause the slimmest among us to weigh hundreds of pounds and all of us to find any movement laboriously difficult, if not impossible. If the world were not tilted just so on its axis, the direct rays of the sun would cause the polar ice caps to melt with the result that much of the planet's land would be flooded. If the earth's atmosphere did not consist of the exact right blend of gases, there would be no way life as we know it could exist.

And so it goes. The earth is delicately balanced in space like a fragile house of cards that can stand up only if built with the utmost care. The fact that it can sustain human life is an incredible miracle.

And if looking outward isn't enough to convince someone of the loving care God has put into his creation, then turn around and take a look inside at the workings of the human body.

Think about it: If all the blood vessels in your body were stretched out end to end, they would go on for some sixty thousand miles—enough to circle the earth more than twice. These blood vessels carry blood to the trillions of cells that make up your body—trillions of cells that work in complete harmony and unity to carry out life's functions.

Take a look at your fingerprints, the tiny grooved patterns on your hands and fingers unlike those found on anyone else's hands and fingers. These fingerprints say that you are a unique individual. No one else is like you. You are a unique creation of a loving God.

Consider the human brain. It enables you to think, to reason, to feel, to hear, to see, to smell, to taste, and to do hundreds of other things. It is vastly more complex than the most advanced computer, and yet God built the first one many thousands of years ago!

Think about the way the organs of your body work together—the lungs breathing in and out, the heart pumping away, the stomach digesting food, and so on. Focus on the heart for a moment. If your heart beats sixty times a minute and you live to be exactly seventy years old, by the time you die your heart will have beat more than 2.2 *trillion* times. I'd like to see the Energizer Bunny keep on going and going and going for that long!

All of these are things we take for granted. We don't go through the day thinking, Boy, I'm sure glad God made this planet just the right size so we don't get crushed by the gravity, or I'm sure grateful I have all these blood vessels in my body, or I sure am blessed that my heart keeps on beating. These things just are, and nobody thinks very much about any of them.

At the same time, if you do stop to think about them, they are truly amazing. They are indicative of God's loving care—those blessings he has built into his creation in behalf of all of his creatures. The plain truth is that anyone who says he has never seen a miracle just isn't looking, because miracles are all around us.

God's care can even be found among the smallest members of his creation. Recently, I read an article on the common honeybee. Sometimes worker bees will venture several miles away from their home hive looking for a good source of pollen. Once one of the bees has found what it's looking for, he returns to his hive and tells the other bees all about it. He does this through a dance with a complicated series of gyrations. One of his moves lets the other bees know which direction to go. Another step lets them know the approximate distance they'll have to travel. And a third movement in the dance lets the others know the size of the find.

All of this from a simple insect! And this same insect, along with his relatives, goes out and dances around in the flowers, causing new life to bloom. Not only that but they also produce honey, which happens to taste great spread on hot buttered biscuits.

Why am I going on about honeybees? Because these amazing little creatures are an indication of the loving way God has built this world to bless us. They are also an example of God's economy—how he uses in a variety of wonderful ways things that seem very simple or mundane to us.

Step One: Ask

I think about the great inventor, George Washington Carver. His example reminds us that one of the ways God blesses us is his willingness to listen to and answer our prayers.

Carver was a pious man who loved the Lord, prayed often, and sought his blessing as well as wisdom. As you probably know, Carver derived more than twenty-five beneficial products out of one small plant—the peanut.

In his later years, Carver once explained that he had prayed and asked God to reveal to him the secrets of the universe. God had replied that he couldn't do that, but he would reveal to Carver the secrets of the peanut. And what amazing secrets that little nut held within its tiny shell!

The Bible assures us that the Lord desires to answer our prayers in a Scripture I call the lucky verse. Why do I call it lucky? Because this helps me remember exactly where it's found—Matthew 7:7. I can remember that not only because seven is God's perfect number but because seven has traditionally been regarded as the "luckiest" number, as opposed to "unlucky" number thirteen. I think we're all very "lucky" to have a God who loves us so much that he wants to answer our prayers.

This verse quotes the words of Jesus, who said: "Ask and it will be given to you; seek and you will find; knock and the door will be opened to you."

George Washington Carver did all of these things. He asked. He sought. He knocked. And God answered his prayer, making him one of the most successful scientists of his day.

But what if he had never asked? What if he had never sought? What if he had never knocked? The point I want to make is that we have to ask for God's blessings. When we do ask him, humbly and sincerely, he will respond. I am more convinced all the time that God loves to answer our prayers. He loves to give us good things. All he's waiting for is for us to ask him.

Please don't misunderstand me. God is not going to flood you with money and jewels and fame just because you ask for them. He will be especially reluctant to give you anything that he sees is going to hurt you. No loving father would give a twelve-year-old son a Corvette and say, "Here you go, son. Happy driving." Instead, such a father would only give his son the things he could

---

*God loves to give us
the things that are good for us.
He delights in giving us
things that will make us
truly happy and joyful.*

handle, the things that would be good for him. God loves to give us the things that are good for us. He delights in giving us things that will make us truly happy and joyful.

Last year, we had a retreat for the staff of Rancho Capistrano Church. It was great to get away for a few days to discuss the future of the church, to pray together, and to be able to develop closer relationships with each other.

At the retreat, Kathy Harris, one of our staff members as well as our pianist and organist, said, "You know, I need more time with my husband. I've been so busy that Pat and I haven't been able to spend good quality time with each other. Would you please pray that we can spend more time together?"

Of course we were all happy to join her in that request.

A month later, at the next staff meeting, Kathy told us that God had really answered our prayer. You see, Kathy usually spends a lot of time playing the organ at various weddings in our area. The month after she made her request about wanting to spend more time with her husband, she didn't have a single wedding. Not one!

At this meeting she told us, "Would you please pray that I'll have some weddings so I can pay my bills?" And then she concluded with this bit of wisdom: "You'd better be careful what you pray for because you'll probably get it."

Naturally, we were happy to pray with Kathy again, and I'm happy to report that the wedding business has picked back up. (But not so much that she's not able to spend time with her husband, too!)

Please don't think for a moment that I'm saying God is malicious or that he won't give us what's best for us. In Kathy's case, I believe he was showing her that he does, indeed, have the capability and the desire to answer her prayers. He was building faith in her, and perhaps in the rest of the church staff, too. The more of God's response to prayers we see, the more we will be able to trust him during those important life-or-death issues.

What's more, I believe the Lord has a sense of humor. I believe he was smiling as he bent down to show Kathy just how involved he really is in her life—just how much he really cares.

God answers prayers. He answers the simple ones, the complex ones, the ones that often seem too big or too remote for us to even talk about. He even answers the prayers that we can't put into words because we just don't know how to pray. God answers these "prayers of the soul," the silent ones deep down in our hearts.

Step Two: Get Yourself into Proper Position

The first thing you have to do if you want to receive a blessing from God is to ask for it. The next step is to get yourself into a position where you can receive it and feel it.

For example, suppose you want to be a stand-up comedian. You might ask God to help you attain your goal. If you sit at home by yourself and wait for people to somehow discover that you are one of the funniest people in the world, I doubt seriously that anything much will happen. You have to look for ways to demonstrate your talent. You might enter local talent contests or go down to the comedy club on amateur night. You would need to seek a position where God could give you this desire of your heart—to be a successful comedian.

Do you see the principle involved?

Before we move on, I want to say again that the purpose of this book is *not* to show you how to get God to start blessing you. He's doing that already. What I hope to do is help you uncover the blessings that God is already pouring out on you. When you fully understand the ways God is blessing you, even when life seems unfair or the cards seem to be stacked against you, that's when you will begin to live in complete peace and contentment.

And there is no better way to live!

3

God's Blessings Last Forever

He was twenty-seven years old. He was hailed as a genius by musical critics throughout the world. He was worth millions of dollars. He was besieged by adoring fans everywhere he went. He was the father of a beautiful baby girl.

Kurt Cobain had everything in the world going for him. But it wasn't enough. And so on an April evening in his luxurious home in Seattle, the leader of the rock group Nirvana put a shotgun to his head, pulled the trigger, and killed himself.

By the standards of the world, Kurt Cobain was a tremendous success. Less than three years ago, no one outside of the Seattle area had ever heard of him or his band. But since that time Nirvana had come out of nowhere to be widely regarded as the world's most influential rock band, selling millions of records in the process. Along the way, Cobain and his bandmates had earned all the trappings of such success. Sadly, for Cobain it wasn't enough, not nearly enough. Yes, Cobain was successful, but he never felt blessed.

> *The blessings the world gives*
> *may last for a season,*
> *but the blessings of God*
> *will endure forever!*

It's an old story. It's happened many times before and, unfortunately, it's sure to happen again. Prosperity and success on the outside are not always the same as prosperity and success on the inside. Exterior success does not alleviate personal pain and anguish; it only eliminates one more excuse for not feeling good about oneself.

For example, consider Howard Hughes. Now there was a fellow who had it all! He was an aeronautical genius, who became the richest man in the world. He was married to more than one of the world's most beautiful women. His was a life full of glamour and elegance.

But that's not how he spent the last few years of his life. Instead, he spent them as a recluse, totally isolated from the world, cut off from everyone he had ever known, without a single friend at his side. His hair was long and scraggly. His fingernails grew until they curved into grotesque shapes. He was the richest man in the world, but he was so bedraggled and unkempt that he looked more like the world's poorest person. By all accounts he was a dirty, ragged bum—with several billion dollars in the bank.

It's ironic, isn't it, how those people we often admire and wish we could trade places with are really miserable down inside their souls? What a contrast to the ways in which God wants to bless us!

The first important thing to remember about the blessings of God is: The blessings the world gives may last for a season, but the blessings of God will endure forever!

The first Psalm puts it this way:

Blessed is the man
  who does not walk in the counsel of the wicked
or stand in the way of sinners
  or sit in the seat of mockers.
But his delight is in the law of the LORD,
  and on his law he meditates day and night.
He is like a tree planted by streams of water,
  which yields its fruit in season
and whose leaf does not wither.
  Whatever he does prospers.

Not so the wicked!
  They are like chaff
  that the wind blows away.
Therefore the wicked will not stand in the judgment,
  nor sinners in the assembly of the righteous.

For the LORD watches over the way of the righteous,
  but the way of the wicked will perish.

You see, God honors those who honor him. He cannot honor those who never speak his name except to use it as a curse word, or those who are always ready to blame him when something goes wrong in their lives but never ready to give him credit or even say, Thank you, God, when things go right.

Have you ever wondered why insurance companies refer to tornadoes, floods, earthquakes, and the like as "acts of God"? I have, and it doesn't seem fair. Sometimes people get caught up in a mindset that sees God's hand only in the bad things and they think that the good things—sunsets and rainbows and bright sunny days—are natural occurrences. I want to assure you that from what I know about God, a beautiful sunset at the end of a beautiful day is much more his act than an earthquake or a hurricane.

I am convinced that the blessings of God are constant, being poured out upon us in great measure on a continuous basis. What we have to do is reach out and take hold of them.

For example, undoubtedly you have a number of electrical outlets in your house. The power is always there, ready for your use. In order to take advantage of it, you have to plug in to it. In the same way, the blessings of God are constant, never-ending, but you've got to "plug in" to them.

The blessings of God are also like a water faucet that is always flowing with cold, clear water. It doesn't matter how much water there might be, your thirst will never be quenched until you take a drink. Again, God is constantly pouring out his blessings, but it's up to us to tap into them.

God's Definition of Success

During the Civil War, one of Abraham Lincoln's generals once told him that the battle was going well because God was on their side. Lincoln replied that it was much more important to know that they had entered the battle on God's side than it was to ask him to be on their side.

What Lincoln meant by this was that some people try to do things backwards. They take a position in life and ask God to bless it. Others do things the right way. They find out what side God is on and then they join him—and this is really the way to do it.

That's how Abraham Lincoln lived his life. If you asked one hundred people at random to name the best president the United States has ever had, I'm sure at least half of them would name Lincoln.

Was Abraham Lincoln blessed? When you look closely at his life, it appears that he wasn't. His many losses are common knowledge. Lincoln failed in business twice. When he was a young man, a woman he loved died. He was defeated in his first attempt to win a seat in the state legislature. He ran for election to the United States Congress twice and lost both times. Then he turned his attention to the Senate, where he suffered two more defeats. Following that, he sought to become vice president. Again, he failed. He saw his young son die. During Lincoln's presidency, the United States was torn apart by civil war. And finally, he was assassinated.

All of this sounds like a roll call of disaster. And yet Abraham Lincoln is widely regarded as one of the greatest Americans who ever lived. If there was ever a man who was a success, if ever there was a man who was blessed, it was "Honest Abe." And I am convinced that the setbacks he suffered as a mortal man are nothing compared to the blessings that will be his throughout all eternity.

God's definition of success is not the same as man's definition. Man has a very limited perspective. While man has trouble seeing much further than next week, or next year at most, God has an eternal perspective.

As an example, I think of a house in my neighborhood that recently underwent a complete renovation. For a long time, it was hard to see what the owners had in mind. I was worried because it looked as if they were going to destroy what had been a beautiful home: This wall was knocked down; that wall was knocked down; the lawn was dug up. The place was a total mess!

But even though it was hard for me to see it for a while, the people who owned this home had long-range plans for it. They knew exactly what they were doing, and they kept looking beyond the temporary messiness to the end result. As it turned out, what they wanted was indeed beautiful. They wound up transforming what had already been a nice home into a showplace.

That's how God looks at things. He sees the end result, and the end result he has in mind for you and me is every bit as beautiful as this house after the renovations had been completed.

Let me give you another difference between the way humans see things and the way the Lord looks at things. It's human nature to look with favor on a man who is ambitious—the fellow who knows what he wants and goes for it. We may not like someone who lives his life always "looking out for number one," but there are certain ways in which we admire him. However, God says that the man who is forever seeking after material blessings will never be satisfied. But the man who seeks first the kingdom of God, who strives to live his life in obedience to God's laws, will be blessed and satisfied.

In his Sermon on the Mount, Jesus said, "Blessed are those who hunger and thirst for righteousness, for they will be filled" (Matt. 5:6). He also said, "Blessed are the pure in heart, for they will see God" (v. 8).

In this same sermon, our Lord said, "Do not lay up for yourselves treasures upon earth, where moth and rust destroy, and where thieves break in and steal. But lay up for yourselves treasures in heaven, where neither moth nor rust destroys, and where thieves do not break in and steal" (Matt. 6:19–20).

The blessings of the world may fade. They may not be everything they were made out to be. But the blessings of God are true and lasting.

What does it mean to be truly blessed?

It means:

- To have peace of mind
- To know you've done the best you can do
- To know your motives are beyond reproach
- To know you are honored in God's eyes
- To have the love and respect of those closest to you
- To love and respect yourself

Blessed Are the Poor in Spirit

There is really only one way for peace and happiness to come into the souls and minds of people, and this is by realizing the truth of Christ's words when he said, "Blessed are the poor in spirit."

Admittedly, I had a pretty difficult time with this verse when I was a child. I had a hard time making sense out of it. In fact, it seemed like a total contradiction. How in the world was I going to be blessed and happy if I walked around all the time with a sad face, frowning and depressed? I thought, *Maybe it means if I'm poor then I'll be happy, so I had better go and give away everything I own. I'd better empty my piggy bank and sell all my toys, and then I'll be happy.* I had failed to understand the meaning of this important verse—that Jesus was not talking about physical poverty.

When the Bible says that the "poor in spirit" will be blessed, what does it mean? It means that the blessed are those people who understand and recognize the divinity and power of God. These are the people who come before him humbly on bended knee and say, I need you today, God. The poor in spirit are not proud and haughty. They do not brag about being self-made, or tell you they never need anybody's help. The poor in spirit are those who openly admit their needs.

In Southern California, we have more than our share of homeless people. They come here in great numbers because it's warm almost all year and they don't have to worry about freezing when they sleep out on the street. California also has its reputation as the "Golden State," and so some come looking for a better life. Obviously, they don't know a whole lot about the present state of California's economy. Unfortunately, many of these people wind up on skid row in cities like Los Angeles, San Diego, and San Francisco.

Now, I'm a big fan of the work most of the missions are doing. They're pulling desperate men and women out of some terrible situations on the streets. They're giving them hot meals, providing a place to sleep, and telling them the important news that God loves them.

But the other day I was talking to a young woman who told me she really didn't have much use for these missions. When I asked her why, she replied, "Because they try to cram God down people's throats."

"I take it you don't believe in God?"

"No, I don't," she said. "And I hate to see these people being told that they need to rely on him. I'd much rather see them being taught that the power lies within themselves to overcome their problems—that they don't need God and they should quit looking for an outside source of help."

As nicely as I could I told her that the very reason most of these people had wound up on the streets in the first place was because they had tried to do things in their own power. Some of them had thumbed their noses at God and said, Hey, God, I don't need you!

I also pointed out to her that belief in God had motivated many of these missions' workers to work in the ghetto. If it wasn't for a desire to reach out and touch the poor with God's love, I doubt that any of them ever would have set foot in the inner city.

The poor in spirit recognize their dependence on God and they are blessed and lifted up because of it. For years, Alcoholics Anonymous has helped people get off drugs and booze by appealing to a higher power. The first of the twelve steps is that the alcoholic recognizes he is helpless against his addiction but that there is a higher power available to help him. Those who rely on God find the help they need. Those who rely on themselves find out, sooner or later, how weak and fallible human flesh is.

The truth is that we all have needs and God wants us to be "poor in spirit" enough to admit our needs and ask for his help.

A friend of mine who works for one of the television networks told me about a hiring experience he had a few years ago. He and his colleagues needed to find a new director for a show they were producing. They had received several résumés and had narrowed the list down to a half-dozen or so people to interview in person. Of these, nobody really "blew their socks off" until the last applicant. The man walked into the room, threw his audition videotape and his résumé on the conference table, looked at his watch, and announced, "Listen, here's my reel. I've got to catch a plane to New York in half an hour so I don't have time to talk. If you want me, fine. You know where you can find me. Let me know."

With that, the man turned and walked out of the room, leaving my acquaintance and his associates staring at each other, mouths wide open.

You guessed it. He was the man they hired. My friend and his colleagues didn't even look at the videotape he'd left them, and they gave his résumé no more than a cursory glance.

However, after only a couple of days they realized that the man didn't know what he was doing. According to my friend, "He was the worst director I ever saw."

Why? Their new employee had never worked as a director at all. He had some experience as an associate director but he needed much more experience before he would be ready to tackle the job of directing, especially for a major network program.

What had happened? This man had wanted success without having to go through the process of learning. He wasn't willing to admit his need, and what he needed was more experience and more knowledge. He managed to get the job he wanted, but he lasted less than a week and ruined his reputation with people who may have been in a position to help him if he had received the experience and the wisdom he needed.

This may be an extreme illustration, but all of us are needy. No matter how much we know, we can always learn more. No matter how much money we make, we always want more. We need more recognition as well and more time for ourselves. We need more hours in the day.

Whatever it is that you or I think we need, we can never really be fulfilled even if we get it. We will always wind up disappointed, because it's not possible to find fulfillment from possessions or recognition or any other similar thing.

True fulfillment comes only when we allow the Spirit of God to re-create in us the presence of his grace and his love. You see, blessings are a gift from God, who says, Here they are, enjoy them.

We can't earn them. We can't buy them. We can't do anything but graciously accept them from the One who wants to give them to us. How? By coming to him humbly and saying, Lord, I'm a poor spirit who needs the gift that you have to offer. I graciously accept it, and I thank you.

Anything the world gives will not last. I don't care what it is, it's going to fade away with time. But the blessings that God gives to those who humble themselves before him and seek his face as well as his favor will last forever.

The World's Way

Not too long ago, I was watching a few innings of a major league baseball game on television. A fellow came up to bat who had been one of the top home-run hitters for several years. Lately, though, he had been struggling, trying to come back from a back injury. It had not been easy. His batting average was low, and he was not hitting many balls out of the park anymore.

At this particular point in the game the bases were loaded. There had been a time when this player would have been able to come through in a clutch situation like this. He probably would have connected for a grand-slam home run, or at the very least he would have hit the ball up the middle and picked up a couple of runs-batted-in. But not this time. This time, he struck out. And, not only did he strike out, he went down looking! With the bat on his shoulder, he took strike three while the ball sailed right down the middle of the plate.

And do you know what the fans did? They booed. Loudly. How many thrills had this man given them over the years? How many times had he come through when the game was on the line, lifting the home team to victory? All of that was forgotten in an instant, and the people who used to cheer him yelled things like, Why don't you retire, you bum?

This is often the kind of blessing that comes from natural success. The world honors you and then it turns around and tries to destroy you. But this is not the way it is with the blessings of God. The blessings he gives to his children last forever. They will not be taken away; they will endure.

Another example of the way the world gives its blessings is the musical group known as New Kids on the Block (or, as they now call themselves, NKOTB).

A few years ago, the boys in this band were the heartthrob of nearly every young girl in America. Their group was one of the biggest merchandising gimmicks going. Not only did they sell millions of records, they also sold millions of T-shirts, posters, and other paraphernalia. There were NKOTB bubblegum cards, curtains, and radios. You name it, and they were selling it. I am convinced that it would have been very difficult to go into the home of any family with a preteenage girl and not find at least some NKOTB merchandise.

But, as they say, that was then and this is now. I saw in the newspaper the other day that NKOTB put out another album, the first in a couple of years. It barely made the charts. After only a few weeks on *Billboard* magazine's list of the best-selling 200 albums, it faded into oblivion.

Strange. Where did the fans go? There had been millions and millions of them. Did they just disappear overnight? Did they come down with amnesia? No, of course not. They had found new heartthrobs. They had discovered new heroes. They didn't care about the old heroes anymore.

Once again, this is a clear illustration of the way of nature, but it's not the way of God. God says, I blessed you yesterday,

I bless you today, and I will bless you tomorrow. He is not fickle or capricious. He won't decide that he wants to bless somebody else now, so he's going to stop blessing you. He doesn't ever stop loving you or desiring to bless you for any reason.

Way Beyond the Balloon

One Saturday morning, when my son, Anthony, was three years old, we were making pancakes. He started singing a song he had learned in Sunday school. (Actually I was making the pancakes, and Anthony was waiting to eat them!)

"Do, Lord, Oh do, Lord, Oh do remember me," he sang out. "Do, Lord, Oh do, Lord, Oh do remember me."

I started teasing him a little bit, singing along with him, "Do remember me . . . way . . . beyond . . . the red. Is that right?"

"No, Daddy. You're wrong."

"Well, is it way beyond the purple?"

"Of course not!"

"Green?"

"No!"

"Orange?"

"No!" He was getting louder now.

"Well, then, what is it?"

"It goes like this, silly." Anthony then sang in a booming voice, "Do remember me, way beyond the balloon!"

My son may have had the words wrong, but his thoughts were right. God is waiting to bless us way beyond the balloon—and way beyond the blue, too. His blessings stretch forever, and they last forever!

As Psalm 1 says, the one who is blessed by God "is like a tree planted by streams of water, which yields its fruit in season and whose leaf does not wither. Whatever he does prospers."

Maybe you realize that you've been looking in all the wrong places for blessings. I'm not saying that if you do, you'll wind

> *The Bible clearly teaches
> that it is all right to give
> while expecting to get back
> a blessing from God
> in one way or another.*

up the way Kurt Cobain did, but you might. At the very least, you'll wind up disappointed and frustrated.

God wants to give you his everlasting blessings. He wants to send his Spirit into your soul to give you the assurance of his love. He wants to give you the conviction of his peace in your life, the reality of his happiness. He wants to grow within you so that his love might overflow to others through you. He wants to fill you with his blessings to the point where you can't help but bless others!

So turn to the Lord. Seek his blessings. He's willing to give.

It's All Right to Give to Get

Sometimes when I talk about the fact that God is willing to bless us, this question comes up: Isn't it wrong to give to God because we expect to get something back from him?

My answer is no, not at all. It's wrong if we really don't care what God thinks or feels, if our entire motivation is selfish. But it is perfectly okay if our own welfare is part of our motivation. In fact, the Bible clearly teaches that it is all right to give while expecting to get back a blessing from God in one way or another.

God's Word is full of God's promises to those who serve him. For example, those who live godly lives in obedience to God's laws are promised that they will be able to live with him forever in paradise. In this regard, God is saying, Give, and you'll get.

Jesus said, "Give, and it will be given to you. A good measure, pressed down, shaken together and running over, will be poured into your lap" (Luke 6:38).

He also said:

> So do not worry, saying, "What shall we eat?" or "What shall we drink?" or "What shall we wear?" For the pagans run after all these things, and your heavenly Father knows that you need them. But seek first his kingdom and his righteousness, and all these things will be given to you as well.
>
> Matthew 6:31–33

In other words, live for God, and he'll bless you.

And there's more:

> "I tell you the truth," Jesus replied, "no one who has left home or brothers or sisters or mother or father or children or fields for me and the gospel will fail to receive a hundred times as much in this present age (homes, brothers, sisters, mothers, children and fields."
>
> Mark 10:29–30

> Behold, I am coming soon! My reward is with me, and I will give to everyone according to what he has done.
>
> Revelation 22:12

Most of us know the story of David and Goliath—how David, a young shepherd boy armed with nothing but a sling and a few pebbles, was able to defeat the giant Goliath, who was well armed and armored too. If you're not familiar with this story, you can find it in the seventeenth chapter of the Old Testament Book of 1 Samuel.

It's a great story, of course, a story about overcoming seemingly insurmountable odds. It's a story about a young man who was willing to put his life on the line to defend his God and his country. It's also about a young man who did something very brave because he knew there would be some nice rewards attached to his deed. We don't talk about this much because we think it detracts somehow from what David did. But I don't think it takes away from his bravery at all. It's another example—a true example—that it's all right to be interested in those blessings attached to giving and obedience.

If you remember the story, you'll recall that the Israelites were at war with their long-time enemy, the Philistines. You may also remember that David wasn't even a soldier. He went to the Israelite encampment to see how his older brothers, who were soldiers, were getting along. Apparently, the battle between the two kingdoms had subsided into a standoff, with the Israelites encamped on one side of the Valley of Elah and the Philistines on the other.

There wasn't really any fighting. Instead, every morning Goliath would come up dressed in his huge armor, let the Israeli soldiers see the sunlight glinting off the blade of his huge sword, and offer to take on the strongest bravest warrior the Israelites could offer. It was the world's first strong-man competition, and it would be winner-take-all. If Goliath won, the Israelite army was to surrender to the Philistines. On the other hand, if Goliath was defeated, the Philistines would surrender.

It wasn't surprising that there weren't any takers among the Israelites. After all, Goliath was about nine feet tall and he was tough! (Imagine Hulk Hogan and Andre the Giant combined into one person, and you're beginning to get the picture!)

If you read 1 Samuel 17:25 you'll find that David's ears really picked up when he heard about the reward King Saul was offering anyone who fought and defeated Goliath. The king was going to give great wealth, his daughter's hand in marriage, and an exemption from paying taxes to the man's family. (I'm not sure which of those offers appealed most to David, but the tax break certainly would have captured *my* attention!)

When David heard the men talking about this generous reward, he turned to some other soldiers and asked them about it. "Have you heard what the king's going to give to whoever defeats this guy?"

They told him what he had already heard.

David wanted to hear it again, so he went and found some different soldiers and asked them the same question: "What will a man get for killing this Philistine and ending his insults to Israel?"

When he heard the same answer once more, David was ready to fight, but not before he had heard three times about the rewards that would come to him if he succeeded. By this time, David was really motivated. He thought about it, and he thought about it, and he came to this conclusion: "Boy, this is really worth it. Besides that, I know I can win because God is with me." Sure enough, David was able to defeat the giant, save his country, and gain some very nice things for himself while doing it.

There is nothing wrong with being motivated by self-interest as long as we are helping people in the process.

Can We Outgive God?

Have you ever heard that it's impossible to outgive God? It's a nice cliché. However, some things become clichés because they're true, and it *is* impossible to outgive God. You just can't do it.

God wants to give you his everlasting blessings. I'm convinced that he wants to show you that you can trust him and that he will honor and bless you when you do.

One of the most dramatic examples of this I've ever encountered involved the man who gave the property on which our church is built. He gave the land not only for the church building but for our retirement center, our retreat center, and our schools. This is some of the choicest, most beautiful land in all of Southern California. This benefactor gave it away because he wanted it used for the glory of God.

This land represented about 50 percent of this man's wealth. The other 50 percent was tied up in prefabricated construction, particularly in an organization called Fleetwood Enterprises. At the time this donor gave the land away, Fleetwood Enterprises stock was selling for around five dollars a share. The *Wall Street Journal* came out with an article predicting the wave of the future in prefabricated construction. Apparently, the article was right on the money because, within the next year, Fleetwood stock went up to forty dollars a share where it split. Two years later, it was back up to forty dollars.

The man thought he was giving away half of his wealth. Instead, he wound up with far more than he had ever had before!

Who controls the construction industry? God does. Who controls the stock market? Again, God does. You *can't* outgive God!

There is a guarantee at work here. God guarantees you that when you get into the position where he can bless you, he will bless you.

Are you in the proper position? If you are, get ready to receive his blessings—blessings that will last forever—blessings that are yours, even when life hurts!

4

Good News!
God Is on Your Side!

Anna is a cancer patient. Once a month, she checks into the local hospital for three days of intensive chemotherapy treatments. These treatments are not easy. They make her terribly sick. They leave her drained and listless. Her hair is falling out in clumps. It seems to take her longer to rebound every time she goes in.

She's had so many blood tests and treatments that the doctor has to poke her arm several times before he can find a healthy vein to use. In addition, doctors have been very blunt with her that there are not likely to be any miracles. The best they can hope for is that the chemotherapy treatments will help to postpone the inevitable, at least for awhile.

What would you do if you were Anna? How would you act toward people? How would you act toward God?

Anna only has about two weeks out of the month where she feels fairly normal. Do you know what she does with this time? She spends a lot of it visiting shut-ins, the elderly, and those who

> *It doesn't matter*
> *who or what is against you*
> *because God is always*
> *on your side.*

are too sick to get out of bed. She rarely lets a day go by that she doesn't send out a card of encouragement to someone with a little note that says, "I appreciate you, and I just wanted to tell you," or "I am praying for you and thinking about you, and I wanted to let you know." In other words, Anna does everything she can to make other people feel better.

She's almost always got a smile on her face and a pleasant greeting or a word of encouragement on the tip of her tongue. Ask her why, and she'll tell you that she feels blessed.

"Blessed? How can you feel blessed?"

"Oh, God has blessed me in so many ways," she says. "I've had so many good things happen to me. And the most important of all is that I'm aware of God's presence in my life. I know he is with me. I know he loves me. What more could I ask for?"

To my way of thinking, there is much more Anna could ask for. But at the same time, I know that she is absolutely right. She has been blessed in many ways, as have we all. And she is aware that having a tangible sense of God's presence in her life really is one of life's very greatest blessings.

This brings me to the second important thing to remember about the blessings that God wants to give you: It doesn't matter who or what is against you because God is always on your side.

I love being a minister. I love telling people the good news that God cares for them and wants only the best for them. I love officiating at weddings and seeing the stars in the eyes of a young man and woman who have found the fulfillment of their dreams in each other's arms. And I love it when a new baby is born into our church family.

But, on the other side of the coin, there are some things about being a minister I could just as soon do without. For example, I could do without the sorrow of sitting by the bedside of someone who is dying but who's not prepared to let go of this life, someone who's scared and fighting to hold on, who is in a panic because the world is slipping from his grasp. And I could definitely do without the sorrow of living through the personal tragedies that befall the people in my flock. Certainly, I'm happy to be there to offer comfort and encouragement when people need it. But at the same time, I hate it when people are hurting.

For example, it is one of the worst things in the world to sit with a family that has just received word that their teenage son has been seriously injured—or even killed—in an automobile accident. The hurt is so bad that there's virtually nothing I can say or do except to sit there and be with them and try to represent God's love.

How is it possible to find the blessings of God in situations like these? For one thing, God promises us that this life is only temporary. To steal a slogan from the Coca-Cola people, life on this planet is not "the real thing." Life goes on beyond the little time we have on this planet of water and clay. People who don't know God don't know this about life. To them, death seems final and devastating. But those who know the Lord understand that death is not the end of anything but rather the transformation from one type of life to another.

Your Pain Won't Last Forever

Those who know God and are comforted by his presence can endure suffering because they understand that it, too, is temporary and that there is a day coming when God will wipe every tear away from the eyes of his people. They are blessed because they realize that what the Bible says is true:

> I consider that our present sufferings are not worth comparing with the glory that will be revealed in us.
>
> Romans 8:18

> He will wipe every tear from their eyes. There will be no more death or mourning or crying or pain, for the old order of things has passed away.
>
> Revelation 21:4

The psalmist David, who was king of Israel, certainly knew his share of bad times. His infant son died. His children's lives were a mess. One of his sons raped one of his daughters, after which another son murdered the boy who raped his sister. And then that son tried to take the kingdom away from him, forcing David and his supporters to flee for their lives.

There were few times in David's life when there wasn't some sort of sinister intrigue swirling about him, and yet David knew the blessed comfort of God's presence in times of trouble. That's why he wrote: "Even though I walk through the valley of the shadow of death, I will fear no evil for you are with me; your rod and your staff, they comfort me" (Ps. 23:4).

The psalmist knew that the Lord was with him and blessing him even in times of deep trouble:

> O Lord, how many are my foes!
>   How many rise up against me!
> Many are saying of me,
>   "God will not deliver him."
>
> But you are a shield around me, O Lord;
>   you bestow glory on me and lift up my head.
> To the Lord I cry aloud,
>   and he answers me from his holy hill.

I lie down and sleep;
  I wake again, because the Lord sustains me.
I will not fear the tens of thousands
  drawn up against me on every side.

Arise, O Lord!
  Deliver me, O my God!
Strike all my enemies on the jaw;
  break the teeth of the wicked.

From the Lord comes deliverance.
  May your blessing be on your people.

Psalm 3

Even in his days of darkest trouble, David knew that the Lord was there for him. He knew he could trust God to deliver him from the clutches of his enemies, whether those enemies were personal or impersonal forces of nature. He knew that God was in control, and as long as that was the case, everything would ultimately work out just the way it was supposed to.

God Remembers You

Do you sometimes feel that God has forgotten about you? He hasn't. As the psalmist also tells us: "All the days ordained for me were written in your book before one of them came to be" (Ps. 139:16).

Not only did God ordain your days before you were born, he also planned how he would bless you. He says: "For I know the plans I have for you, . . . plans to prosper you and not to harm you, plans to give you hope and a future" (Jer. 29:11). Think of it! God has plans to give you peace and a future filled with hope. He wants to see your soul prosper.

I'm sure you remember the story of Noah, and God's commandment to build an ark because a great flood was going to come upon the earth. The Bible tells us that, while Noah and his family were safely inside the ark,

Every living thing that moved on the earth perished—birds, livestock, wild animals, all the creatures that swarm over the earth, and all mankind. Everything on dry land that had the breath of life in its nostrils died. Every living thing on the face of the earth was wiped out; men and animals and the creatures that move along the ground and the birds of the air were wiped from the earth. Only Noah was left, and those with him in the ark.

Genesis 7:21–23

Even though Noah, his wife, and their children were safe, those must have been terrible times, bouncing along on top of the waves deep inside the darkness of a monstrous wooden ship, knowing that all life on the outside had been destroyed, wondering what was going to happen next.

And then, the first verse of the eighth chapter of Genesis says, "But God remembered Noah . . ." This doesn't imply that God had forgotten about Noah and his family. It means that he constantly remembered Noah. God hadn't forgotten about those people in the ark for a single moment. He was going to be with them, rescue them, and bring them out to begin life anew in a world that had been cleansed from all evil and lawlessness.

Scholars of the ancient Hebrew text will tell you that this particular verse stands at the exact center of the story. To ancient Hebrew readers, this would have been the central thought of the text. It was not an afterthought nor an incidental statement. It was a statement that stood out, that captured the reader's attention.

God hadn't forgotten Noah, and God hasn't forgotten you either. He is there, wherever you are, trying to hold your hand and let you know he cares.

As the psalmist says:

Where can I go from your Spirit? Where can I flee from your presence? If I go up to the heavens, you are there; if I make my bed in the depths, you are there. If I rise on the wings of the dawn, if I settle on the far side of the sea, even there your hand will guide me, your right hand will hold me fast.

Psalm 139:7–10

We Remember God

On a blustery November day in the year 1873, a man named Horatio Spafford was waiting for word from his wife and four daughters, who were on a ship bound for Europe. Spafford had stayed behind in the United States due to pressing business, but his plan was to join them as soon as he could.

Now, it was long past time when he should have received word from them. As the hours and days went by, the man became increasingly worried. There were storms at sea and dangerous waves pounding the coastline.

Finally word arrived, but it was not the word he wanted to hear. There had been a collision at sea. The ship carrying his wife and children had sunk to the bottom of the Atlantic in a matter of minutes. His wife had been rescued, but 226 people had drowned including all four of his children.

Spafford was devastated, as any husband and father would be. Yet he was a man who had been walking hand-in-hand with God for many years. He had experienced God's deliverance in times of trouble. He had felt the closeness of communion with his Lord. His faith had been built up over the years to the point where he understood that nothing that happened in this life—no matter how devastating or how terrible—could begin to compare with the happiness and the joy waiting on the other side of eternity.

And so it was that Horatio Spafford took out pen and paper and wrote the words to the hymn many of us know so well:

> When peace, like a river, attendeth my way,
> When sorrows like sea billows roll—
> Whatever my lot, Thou hast taught me to say,
> It is well, it is well with my soul.

Here was a man who had sorrow far greater than most of us could imagine, but he knew the presence of God in his life. He knew that God was blessing him even in the midst of the deepest tragedy. And he realized, because he knew God, that whatever separation and loss he felt was only temporary. Reunion was—and is—sure to come.

To someone who doesn't believe in God or who had only a tenuous relationship with the Almighty, this man's trust in the face of such overwhelming loss and pain might be difficult to understand. The story might even sound trite or simplistic. But, you see, when you choose to build and nurture your relationship with God, then you can know that he will be there to help you through the tough times that blow into your life. Those who don't really take the time to get to know God in an intimate way may not be able to hang onto him through times of real pain and loss. But those who *do* know him will be walking on top of the waves, never even thinking about the possibility of sinking!

God Is Your Compass

If you know me, you know that I love to get out on the ocean. It's a means of escape—a way in which I can get away from some of the pressures of life and recharge my batteries. It's not

> *When tribulation comes your way— or persecution or frustration— remind yourself that God is with you and that he is blessing you right now!*

uncommon for me to get out there ten, twenty, or even fifty miles offshore.

Do you know what you see when you're that far away from land? You see water—lots and lots of water, as far as you can see out to the horizon. Sometimes it's hard to tell where the water ends and the sky begins. And sometimes, you get very confused. It's easy to start wondering which way the shore is.

When my kids are on the boat, I'll ask them which way they think we need to go to get back to land. Invariably, they'll point in the wrong direction. Sometimes they're just making a wild guess. Other times, they feel confident they're pointing in the right direction, but they aren't.

"No, you're wrong," I tell them. "The shore is that way."

"No, it's not. It's right over there."

"I'm sorry but it's *that* way."

And I'm always right.

Does this mean that I'm the world's best sailor? No, but it does mean that I'm the one with the compass!

Sometimes I have to say, "I feel just like you do. I think we need to go that way to get back to shore. But my compass here tells me I'm wrong." And I know that when it comes to choosing which to trust—my feelings or my compass—I always trust the compass.

It is easy to get lost out there on the sea of life. When trouble comes your way, however, you have a compass. Even though you seem adrift on an ocean of troubles, you can know that God is with you, looking out for you and taking care of you. Keep your eyes on the Lord, and he will get you safely to shore.

When tribulation comes your way—or persecution or frustration—remind yourself that God is with you and that he is blessing you right now!

Always remember that God loves you. Paul said it this way in Romans 8:38: "Neither death nor life, neither angels nor demons, neither the present nor the future, nor any powers, neither height nor depth, nor anything else in all creation, will be able to separate us from the love of God that is in Christ Jesus our Lord." Did you get that? *Nothing* can separate you from God's love.

Remember, too, that you are a unique, prized, and loved person and that God has a place for you in his kingdom. Isn't it good to know that God not only loves you but has a place for you?

When I was in junior high school, my father and I went to Washington, D.C. We were walking down the street when we stopped to watch some construction work on the Washington Cathedral. One of the men was chiseling and shaping a stone. I asked him why he was going to so much trouble with one little stone.

"I'm shaping it so it'll fit right there." He pointed to a place in the wall where one stone was missing. The worker couldn't shove the stone in there any old way; he had to shape and mold it until it fit perfectly.

God is shaping us, too. He has the perfect place for us in his eternal plan, but he must get us to the point where we fit perfectly. He is chipping away, and this sometimes hurts. But the end result will be the blessing of taking our special place in God's kingdom.

Trust in God. He will bring you safely through the storm. He is blessing you right now.

One of the most important ways he's belssing you is by offering you peace of mind. You can have it right now. All you have to do is reach out and take it. Let me explain.

5

God Offers Peace in the Midst of Turmoil

It was a fun party, and I was having a wonderful time. There was laughter and music and food and good conversation, and what made it even better was that it was for an excellent cause. We were there to raise money to help abused children through Child Help USA.

It was early in the evening when my wife, Donna, tapped me on the arm and pointed to a nearby table. I was delighted to see that she was gesturing in the direction of some friends, people we like very much but, for various reasons, hadn't seen for quite a while. We got up from our table and went over to talk to them.

"Bill, Laura, it's so good to see you," I said.

"It's great to see you, too." They smiled back at us.

This is a couple I've always admired. Whenever I hear the expression "having it all together," these are the people I think of. Bill's a good guy: pleasant, positive, and clever. He has an excellent job. What's more, he has made some wise investment choices and is doing well financially. Laura is one of the most beautiful women I've ever seen—a stunning beauty. They seem to be a truly blessed, truly happy couple. And to make their happiness complete, Laura had given birth to a healthy baby boy fifteen months earlier.

"How are you doing?" I asked.

"We're great," came the reply.

"And how's the baby?"

Laura kept smiling as if everything was fine. Then all of a sudden, a huge tear rolled down her cheek, and she buried her head in her hands and began to sob. Bill reached over and put his arm around her.

Donna and I stood there waiting, feeling helpless. "What's wrong?" Donna asked.

Finally, Laura regained her composure and told us. "Please pray for us," she said. "We just found out that our baby is a dwarf."

"I'm sorry," I said.

"That's not the worst part. The doctors don't think he's going to live very long."

"Why?"

She went on. "In most dwarfs the internal organs grow but their chest cavities don't. Eventually their organs get choked by their chest cavities and their ribs, and they suffocate."

"Isn't there something you can do? Some kind of operation or something?"

Bill shook his head. "Medical science can't do a thing."

No one said anything for a few seconds, but I knew what we were all thinking—medical science might not be able to do anything for their son, but God could. He's not bound by the limitations of science, medical or any other kind. As the Bible tells us, "with God all things are possible" (Matt. 19:26).

As the music, laughter, and conversation swirled around us, we held hands and prayed for that little boy. We asked God to reach down in his mercy and supernaturally touch the child, enabling him to grow normally like any other child.

When we finished, Laura looked around with a smile on her face. "I feel so peaceful right now."

We could each feel the peace of God. It had flooded over us like waves of warm soothing water. His presence was obvious. There was a reassurance, as if he were saying, I'm here. Don't be afraid. None of us had anything supernatural happen. Nobody heard a voice saying, I've heard your prayer, and I'll give you what you've asked for. But we all had the feeling that God was there, and that was enough.

I'd like to end this story by telling you that this couple's little boy is fine, that there was an immediate change in his condition, and that doctors are baffled. I can't, but this doesn't mean that God's hand is not at work in his life. This incident happened fairly recently, and enough time hasn't passed to tell whether the child will survive to adulthood. It is in God's hands.

> *God will bless you*
> *with his peace*
> *if you ask him for it.*
> *And this peace*
> *will keep you feeling*
> *safe and secure*
> *even in the worst moments*
> *of the storm!*

But I also believe that whatever happens to him, God is in charge of the situation because God is love personified. He will work it out for the good of everyone concerned. I also believe that Bill and Laura are being blessed by God's peace in the midst of what are obviously trying times. What's more, I not only believe, but know that God is ready and willing to give you the same type of peace right now. God will bless you with his peace if you ask him for it. And this peace will keep you feeling safe and secure even in the worst moments of the storm!

When Things Are Looking Down, Look Up!

The Bible refers to the peace of God as the peace that "transcends all understanding" (Phil. 4:7). This means that you can be totally calm and peaceful no matter how life looks at the moment. God really is in charge, and he really does love you, more than you could possibly understand.

When things are looking down for you, you can always look up. In the midst of the hurt and the pain in your life, God is reaching down and blessing you.

Psalm 29:11 says, "The LORD gives strength to his people; the LORD blesses his people with peace."

And Philippians 4:7 echoes those words when it says, "And the peace of God, which transcends all understanding, will guard your hearts and your minds in Christ Jesus."

What we felt in that banquet hall, in the midst of that party, was the peace that transcends all understanding. Anyone looking at it from a purely practical viewpoint might say, How in the world can you feel peaceful? That little boy is sick. He might die! But even with such a reality, God's presence can bring peace and reassurance.

Your understanding says, This is terrible. I can hardly face up to it! But your spirit says, God is here. He's in charge. I can rest in his will and enjoy the moment. I can thank him for the gift of life he has given me today.

When You're Too Wound Up to Wind Down

I would be among the first to admit that these are hectic days we live in. It's not always easy to find peace and contentment in the midst of our hurry-up, can't-slow-down world.

My son has a toy helicopter that operates by a wind-up spring. You set it on the ground and watch the rotor spin as the little toy moves across the floor.

If you know little boys, you know that fast is never fast enough.

"Faster, Daddy. I want it to go faster," he says.

"That's as fast as it will go," I tell him.

But Anthony isn't satisfied. He figures if he gives the spring a few extra twists, the helicopter will probably have a good shot at lifting off the ground. So that's what he decides to do: twist, and twist, and then twist some more. You know what happens. Anthony gives that spring one twist too many, and—sproinggg— it snaps in two!

Do you ever feel like this is about to happen to you: One more twist and the springs that bind you are going to snap in about a dozen places? Well, God is there saying, Let me help you. Let me give you my peace. As 1 Peter 5:6–7 says, "Humble yourselves, therefore, under God's mighty hand, that he may lift you up in due time. Cast all your anxiety on him because he cares for you."

What we have to understand and believe is that God always knows what we need, and he is always ready to give that to us. But what we need may not be the same as what we want. And that's where some of us have difficulty.

When Anthony told me that he wanted his helicopter to go faster and I told him no, he didn't understand. He persisted and wound up breaking his toy. That's what you might expect from Anthony because, after all, he's only a little boy. But we can all be like that at times.

I want that!

God says, No, it really wouldn't be good for you. I'm sorry.
But I want it!
I told you it would hurt you!
I want it now!
Maybe I'm talking to you, and maybe I'm not. Maybe I'm talking only to myself. The truth is we can all act like petulant children sometimes, because we just don't see things the same way God does. This is when we get into trouble—when we try to tell God how to do things. He knows best. That's why he's God! And because he is God, he is unfolding the universe (and that includes your life and mine) in exactly the right way.

If you are bound up with the cares and worries of life, then God is saying to you, Relax. I'm in charge here.

Remember the popular saying, "Let go and let God"? I think we ought to revive this. If we don't learn to let go and let God, some of us are going to snap like the spring in my little boy's helicopter.

When you get to the point where you are saying, I can't, remember that he can. And let him! His power is far greater than yours or mine, and he's willing to use that power to help you.

When you come to understand that the Lord really is in charge and that he wants only the best for you, his peace will surround you.

There is a parable about a man who was talking to God, and he said, "Oh, Lord, how much is a thousand years in your sight?"

And the Lord replied, "Ah, a thousand years is but a second to me."

The man said, "Oh, Lord, how much is a million dollars in your sight?"

"It is but a penny," was God's reply.

"Then," said the man, "can you bless me with a penny?"

"Certainly," said the Lord, "in just a second."

While God is blessing us all the time, he is not blessing us if he acts like some magic genie who has nothing better to do than run errands for us and grant our wildest wishes. If that were so, the world would be made up of 5.8 billion minigods, called people, creating total chaos and anarchy.

Everyone has prayer requests, and we lift them to God. But God, in his wisdom and knowledge, knows what is going to bless us and what is going to hurt us. Sometimes we pray and God says yes, and we immediately feel his blessings. We see his hand move in response to our prayers, and we know that he is alive and that he cares about us. But then there are times when we say, Oh, God, why don't you give me this? The gift doesn't come, and we can't understand why he does not bestow upon us what we believe is so critically important. In his wisdom, God knows that we need to grow, that we're not prepared for what we're asking for, that it might damage or even kill us.

I am convinced that there is never a prayer that God doesn't answer. Sometimes he answers by saying no. I can't always tell you why he says no. Sometimes it doesn't seem fair or right, but I know that I don't see things from his vantage point so I have to release my own desires and say, God, do what you want to do because I know it's the best thing anyway. When I give my desires up to God in this way, his peace floods through my soul. Giving control of our lives to God is the most critical thing we can do to feel his blessings right now.

> *Giving control*
> *of our lives to God*
> *is the most critical thing*
> *we can do to feel his blessings*
> *right now.*

If You Want Peace, Quit Fighting!

If you are striving to be a peacemaker, you can be sure that God is pouring out his blessings upon you, whether or not those blessings will be seen clearly this side of eternity. As Jesus said in his Sermon on the Mount, "Blessed are the peacemakers, for they will be called sons of God" (Matt. 5:9).

God wants us to be bridge builders. He wants us to enter every situation and every relationship in a constructive way. I often pray that God will help me do this. I urge you to do the same: Lord, help me always to seek to build up and not to tear down, to be constructive and never destructive.

Those of us who know the peace of God need to help transform this high-tech society of ours into a high-touch society. Many mental health professionals agree that human beings need several hugs every day to function at optimum levels. They need to be touched and cared for and told that they matter. We need to pray that God will fill us so full of his peace and his love that they will overflow onto those we come into contact with everyday.

Have you ever had a friend who always had an encouraging word, a smile, or a tender touch that told you they cared? That's what it means to be a peacemaker. Remember Anna? Even though she struggles against cancer, she does what she can to bring love and kindness to others. She is a peacemaker, and in the midst of turmoil she lives a life of quiet peace. Those who strive for peace, receive his peace.

However, the world doesn't always understand the peacemakers. If you are one, you'll probably have your motives questioned. You'll come up against people who don't want peace because they like to bicker and fight. (Some people nurse grudges so long that the grudges grow into full-blown anger and resentment.) You may be told to chill out or that the conflict is none of your business. You may even be hurt in some way.

Just the other day, there was a story in my local newspaper about a young man who tried to be a peacemaker and paid with his life. Two men were fighting, and he attempted to stop them. He hadn't been involved in the argument at all. One of the men pulled out a gun and shot him three times, killing him. The friends of the dead man said that it was just like him to try to make peace.

In this world it seems that the avocation of peacemaker can often be a dangerous one.

For example, I think of another peacemaker by the name of Martin Luther King.

His attempts to make peace were not between individuals, but between entire races. In a time when other black leaders were advocating the use of violence to obtain equal rights, and some were preaching the superiority of the African race, Dr. King was preaching peace, brotherhood, and non-violence.

Surely Dr. King was a great leader in his people's fight for freedom and equality, but every bit as much as that, he was a peacemaker. And he, too, paid with his life, shot down in his prime as he stood on the second-floor balcony of a Memphis hotel.

At this point, you might be saying, Now, wait a minute. You've been telling us that God blesses peacemakers, but then you tell us about two men who paid with their lives for their efforts to make peace. That doesn't sound much like being blessed to me!

Being blessed doesn't mean you will physically live forever. It doesn't mean you'll live to a ripe old age. We must never lose sight of the fact that life is a gift from God. Every day is a gift from him and a day he can use us to make peace and to make our lives count.

If we were to put our lives on a historical timeline from the first day to the apocalypse, it would be nothing more than a speck. If we lived ten years or one hundred, the size of the speck would hardly be visible even under a microscope. But when we understand the magnificent gift and promises of God for our eternal existence, the speck becomes the starting point for the life that lasts forever, of a life made significant by God's dwelling in it.

I believe in the blessings of God, and I believe in a resurrection. I believe that God's blessings far transcend anything that can happen to us while we live in the flesh. I also believe that you can experience God's greatest blessings even in the middle of what seems to be personal failure and tragedy.

I do not want you to come away from this book thinking that I am saying that those who live in God's blessings will never experience troubles. You will have tough times. There will always be problems. But that doesn't mean God is not blessing you. In the midst of pain we can still see God's blessings when we look for them. For example, look at Acts 7:54–59. This is the Bible's account of the execution of Stephen, one of the first Christian martyrs. The Bible tells us that even as Stephen's accusers were hurling huge rocks at him, he looked up to heaven and saw the glory of God. As the rocks were bouncing off him, he cried out, "Look, . . . I see . . . God" (v. 56).

There can be no greater blessing than to see God, and this was the very honor bestowed on this dying man. God was welcoming him home. At that moment, I am convinced that God's arms were wrapped around Stephen. He was being cared for, comforted, and, yes, even protected from the torture his enemies were attempting to inflict upon him. In the face of death, Stephen was being blessed.

The Power of Prayer

God will give you his peace if you'll just ask for it. The power of prayer is amazing, because it can break through all the barriers we've put up—the fences and walls and deadbolts. Once you've found the peace of God through prayer, you can start giving it away to others. It's easy to do. It's just a matter of sharing it with someone who needs it.

Think about it. How many people do you know who need a prayer, who desperately need to know that God loves them and is blessing them now? Maybe it's your husband or wife.

Your boss. Your next-door neighbor. Your brother or sister, or coworker. Your friend from down the street. The person who sits by himself in church on Sunday. It can be anyone. With God's blessings, you can help others feel his blessings through prayer. So pray for them and pray with them.

Have you ever listened to someone's troubles and then said, "I'll pray for you"? Did you then forget about it before you got around to it? You meant well, but other things came along and you simply forgot. You can remedy this by praying immediately, wherever you are. As Clem Stone says, *"Do it now!"*

This is what I did with Bill and Laura. I'm not suggesting that you should make a big show of it. If you don't want to be conspicuous, pray with your eyes open. Look into the other person's eyes. You don't have to close your eyes every time you pray. Softly offer your petitions and praise to God. When you pray for another, the prayer draws both of you closer to God as well as to each other. It invites the peace of God into the relationship.

Also, simply telling someone I'm praying for you, can bring a measure of God's peace. Let the person know what you know: God loves him and is blessing him.

God is blessing you right now by giving you the strength and ability to bring his peace into your family, neighborhood, and workplace, through your heart attitude and your prayers. What an opportunity!

We've seen that God is giving you the kinds of blessings that will last forever. He is truly reaching out to bless you even when life hurts. And do you know what else he wants to do? He wants to set you free from sin and guilt. I'll tell you how and why in chapter 6.

6

More Good News: God Doesn't Hold a Grudge

Blessed is he
   whose transgressions are forgiven,
   whose sins are covered.
Blessed is the man
   whose sin the LORD does not count against him
   and in whose spirit is no deceit.
                              Psalm 32:1–2

The young man's shoulders were drooping as he neared his hometown. The closer he got, the more his shoulders drooped. This wasn't because the man was tired, although he had been on the road for days now—and he *was* tired and ragged and hungry. His shoulders were low because he knew what lay ahead: humiliation and rejection. He knew he wasn't going to be welcomed home.

As far as the neighbors were concerned, this young man had publicly rejected his family, his community, and even his country. He was a traitor, a radical, a hippie. While the other young men of the community had stayed home and worked hard to help support their families, he had gone off in search of nothing more than a good time. He had, in effect, thumbed his nose at the mores of his community and scorned the things it believed in. He had trampled its values beneath his feet. In the process, he had squandered a bundle of his family's money, and now that he was broke and hungry, he was crawling back asking for a second chance. The young man didn't figure anyone was going to be too happy to give him a second chance, but he knew he didn't have a choice. This was his last hope.

What could he expect? He'd probably get roughed up or at least verbally abused by the village tough guys: Hey, look who's come crawling back! Somebody, step on it before it gets away! They might not hurt him physically but then again, they might. His reception probably wasn't going to be much friendlier from the community's "proper" residents, either.

Even his own father probably wouldn't welcome him home with open arms. More than likely, his father was going to keep him waiting outside on the porch for several hours while he thought about whether to let him inside. Then there was no guarantee that his father would ever be gracious. It was entirely within the realm of possibility that he would never even agree to meet with his son. After all, the boy had asked for his inheritance in advance, in effect saying, I can't wait for you to die, Dad. I want the money now. And then he had gone off and blown it.

The young man heaved a heavy sigh. *Maybe I made a mistake in coming home,* he thought. *I must be a fool to think he'd have me back.*

No sooner had he thought this than he looked up and saw someone running toward him: a small, solitary figure, coming along the dirt road, his garments blowing in the breeze, small dust clouds kicking up behind him as he ran.

Could it be? Naw . . . But it was! It was his father. And he had his arms wide open in a gesture of welcome!

The next thing he knew, the young man was being swept up in the old man's arms. The father was crying and kissing his son and saying how glad he was to see him. And then the son cried, too, and held his father for dear life, wondering how it was possible that his father could love him so much.

You've probably heard the story before. It's the parable of the prodigal son, a story Jesus told in Luke 15:11–32 to illustrate the love that God has for his children. The only problem is that most of us have heard this story so many times that it has lost its impact.

We do not fully understand the ways in which the son had insulted his father or rejected his heritage and his homeland. We don't understand that, by forgiving his son so easily, the father was risking looking weak and spineless in front of his neighbors. (At the very least, they expected him to subject the son to a public whipping, thus reasserting his authority and obtaining retribution for the way his son had treated him.)

I imagine that some of his neighbors rolled their eyes and thought, What about retribution? when they saw the way he forgave the boy. That's because human nature says things like,

> *It doesn't matter what you have done.*
> *If God declares you not guilty, then you aren't guilty.*

Don't get mad, get even. Human beings tend to keep score; they worry about giving tit for tat.

Thankfully, God's nature is not the same as human nature. Through this parable, Jesus gives us a clear picture of God's willingness and ability to forgive us when we do things we shouldn't do. He is *always* ready to forgive, always ready to receive us home, always ready to meet us more than halfway.

This is another one of the ways God is blessing you right now—by forgiving and forgetting your sins whenever you sincerely ask him to forgive you. It doesn't matter what you have done. If God declares you not guilty, then you aren't guilty.

God's mercy is large enough to cover anything and everything you can possibly do. Yes, God has given us certain rules and told us to live by them, but when we don't, he is quick to forgive us anyway. Not only does he forgive the sins of the past, he also provides a way to receive forgiveness for the transgressions of today and tomorrow.

I once heard a story—the man who told it to me said it was true—about a father who went to great lengths to teach his young sons about the love of God. The man went out of town on a business trip and, before leaving, carefully instructed his boys not to touch an expensive piece of computer equipment he had in his study.

Human nature being what it is—and kids being kids—the dad hadn't been gone for more than fifteen minutes when the boys were in that room, rolling around on the floor with the piece of sensitive high-tech equipment. Of course, they broke it, and there was nothing to do but await the punishment they knew was coming.

When the father returned, they fearfully reported to him what they had done and braced for the worst. Sure enough, the dad marched them up to their bedroom. He explained that because they had disobeyed his orders, they had to be punished. And then, he told them that he was prepared to take the punishment for them. The father took off his belt, leaned over the bed, and told his boys that he wanted them to spank him!

"But, Dad," the oldest said, "we can't do that!"

"You have to," he replied. "You knew that if you disobeyed me, you'd be punished. The only thing that's different is that I'm willing to take your place."

When their father could not be dissuaded, his young sons spanked him, though halfheartedly and with big tears running down their cheeks. After this, he sat them down and explained to them what he had done.

"What I did in taking the punishment you deserved was the same thing God does for us all," he told them. "We break his laws, and we deserve to be punished for that. But then God says, I'll take your place. I'll take upon myself the punishment you deserve."

This dad's explanation for what happened was something that his children could understand. It was a clear presentation of what Christ had done on the cross when he took the sins of the world upon himself. And this is one of the things that makes Christianity unique among the world's religions. The central truth of Christianity is that Christ himself paid for our sins. By accepting his payment on our behalf, we can obtain forgiveness.

This story shows one caring father's method for explaining a complex subject to his children. It's not profound, I realize, but in its simplicity, it drives home the way God does bless us when he forgives our transgressions. When God forgives us, he gives us the ability to forgive ourselves, to know that the wrong things we've done in the past really don't matter anymore. He speaks to the heart of the person who is living under a cloud of guilt and shame and says, Forget about it. It doesn't matter any more. I've forgotten all about it, and I want you to do the same.

The Bible talks about being justified. Romans 3:23–24 says: "All have sinned and fall short of the glory of God, and are justified freely by his grace through the redemption that came by Christ Jesus."

What does justified mean? As an old-time preacher explained, it means "just-as-if-I'd" never sinned. When God says you are justified, you really are justified. He no longer remembers you did anything wrong.

There is nothing you can do that is beyond the grace of God to forgive. In Isaiah 1:18 God says, "Though your sins are like scarlet, they shall be as white as snow; though they are red as crimson, they shall be like wool."

What God is saying here is that you may look at your life and see the wrong things you've done, and they may stand out like the scarlet "A" that Hester Prynne was forced to wear in Nathaniel Hawthorne's *Scarlet Letter.* However, when God forgives, he washes your sins so clean you can't even see them anymore.

It's like those laundry commercials where the homemaker is washing the dirtiest pile of laundry you've ever seen. There are all those bloodstains (making you wonder exactly what it is that dad does for a living), grease stains, food stains, you-name-it stains. She puts the whole pile into the washer, pours in the detergent, and a few seconds later—voila! She takes out the whitest, brightest, cleanest shirts, pants, and underwear you've ever seen.

You don't have to be weighed down by guilt and regret. You don't have to go around feeling bad about what you've done. You don't have to worry if God is willing to forgive you.

The psalmist assures us:

As far as the east is from the west, so far has he removed our transgressions from us. As a father has compassion on his children, so the LORD has compassion on those who fear (respect) him; for he knows how we are formed, he remembers that we are dust.

Psalm 103:12–14

You see, God understands our frailties. He knows we are prone to stumble. He is wise enough not to expect us to be perfect, and he is compassionate enough to forgive us when we aren't perfect.

Learning to Fly the Flag of Grace

At the beginning of this chapter, we looked at the first two verses of the thirty-second Psalm.

Now let's take a look at the next four verses:

> When I kept silent,
>   my bones wasted away
>   through my groaning all day long.
> For day and night
>   your hand was heavy upon me;
>   my strength was sapped
>   as in the heat of summer.
> Then I acknowledged my sin to you
>   and did not cover up my iniquity.
> I said, "I will confess
>   my transgressions to the Lord"—
> and you forgave
>   the guilt of my sin.
>   Psalm 32:3–5

Many lessons can be drawn from these verses. The first is that we need to learn to fly the flag of grace. Let me explain.

A few years ago, everywhere you went in a country called the Soviet Union, you saw the same red flag, the one with the hammer and sickle design on it. That flag symbolized the triumph of communism, and the unity of workers everywhere in communist society.

But then as communism began to unravel, the Soviet Union also began to unravel. There never was much of a union there to begin with; the Soviet Union was a collection of diverse and sometimes antagonistic states held together by the strong arm of Mother Russia. And so, as communism collapsed, one of these countries after another began to proclaim its independence: Lithuania, Georgia, Khazikstan, the Ukraine, and so on. All over that part of the world, the hammer and sickle was coming down and new flags were going up, flags that represented freedom and independence. The people in those countries were tired and angry because of the way communism had kept them in bondage for so many years. They didn't want to look at that hammer and sickle anymore. Even in Russia, the symbol of communist rule was pulled down and trampled underfoot.

In the same way, the psalmist talks about how he groaned and how his strength was sapped as in the heat of summer. The flag of guilt and condemnation was flying over his heart, and until, with God's help, that flag had been pulled down and replaced with the flag of grace, David was going to be sad and miserable.

Take a look at yourself and see if you can figure out what flag is flying over your heart and mind. Is it the flag of guilt or the flag of grace? If it's guilt, ask the Lord to help you pull it down and replace it with the flag of freedom and independence he offers through his love and grace. This is one of the ways God is willing to bless you right now!

A second thing we can learn from this psalm is the importance of confession—the way to obtain the flag of grace.

What does it mean to confess? It means that you admit to yourself the exact nature of what you've done wrong, and quit making excuses for yourself. It means that you admit your faults to God *and* to another human being, someone you trust implicitly, whether that someone is a pastor, priest, or a best friend.

Acknowledging our sin to God is an important step in obtaining his forgiveness. Both the Old and New Testaments stress the importance of confession over and over again. It was only when David confessed his transgression that the Lord forgave the guilt of his sin.

Why is confession so important? Doesn't God already know what we've done anyway? Of course he does. But he wants us to openly acknowledge our shortcomings. He knows we need to confess because it's good for our souls. There is an emotional

---

God wants to forgive you.

---

release that comes from openly admitting to God the sins we have committed. It is also an admission of the fact that we need his grace and his mercy as well as an acknowledgment of the relationship that God wants and expects us to have with him.

A third lesson we can learn from these verses of Psalm 32 is the danger of trying to hide our sins. Remember what we said a few moments ago—God knows what we've done already; trying to hide anything from him is absurd.

Have you ever seen a little child who thought that he was hiding from you when he closed his eyes? He thinks that when he can't see you, you can't see him either. Sometimes this is the way people are with God. They think that if they refuse to look at their sins, the Lord won't see them either. But he does see them. And so does the person who's pretending that everything is fine. Deep down inside, that person knows something is wrong. He has a feeling that something just isn't right but is afraid to face up to it.

There is a release and relief that comes from pouring out your heart to God. If you keep things bottled up inside, sooner or later infection will set in and spread throughout your being.

God wants to forgive you. God doesn't want you to live in bondage. He wants to bless you by forgiving your sins, and he wants to do it right now.

God doesn't want to be angry with us. He's not the type to say, Well, you really hurt my feelings so you're going to have to beg me to forgive you. He won't pout and say, I'll think about forgiving you, but I'm not too sure if I really want to. He is like the father in the parable of the prodigal son, who came running with arms wide open because he couldn't wait to forgive his son and welcome him back home. Our heavenly Father is always ready and willing to forgive and delighted to do so, too. And he'll do it the moment we ask.

Suppose you did something for which you are really ashamed. Perhaps you cheated on your income tax, and it is really bothering your conscience. You get down on your knees and say, "God, I'm so sorry that I cheated on my income tax. I really feel bad about it. Please forgive me." How does God respond? "I forgive you." He is a lot more willing to forgive than good old Uncle Sam!

Is Your Life Working?

I have heard Dr. Norman Vincent Peale talk about the time he wandered into a tattoo parlor. He wasn't looking for a tattoo. He was just curious. As he looked around at the different slogans and symbols people could choose, one in particular caught his eye. It said "born to lose."

"Excuse me," Dr. Peale asked the owner of the shop. "Do people really choose to have this printed on their bodies?"

"Oh, sure," came the answer. "Lots of people like that one."

"I don't understand. Why?"

"Why?" the owner repeated. "They choose to have it printed on their arms because it's already printed in their minds."

Can you imagine that? Thinking that you are destined to lose in life? God hasn't created anyone to be a loser. He wants us all to be winners. In fact, he is willing to help us change from losers into winners by forgiving all the mistakes we've ever made and giving us a clean slate and a chance to start over.

Have you ever seen the children's poster that says, "I know I'm somebody special because God don't make no junk"? The grammar is not great, but the thought behind it is terrific. Every human being is created in God's image, and this means every human being is meant to be a winner.

If your life isn't working the way you want it to work, then a change is definitely in order. It very well may start with the forgiveness of your transgressions and a new start in life. If you're one of those people who think they should be wearing a big bold "born to lose" tattoo, then let God bless you and help you change your attitude about yourself.

Let's go back to Psalm 32 and read the sixth and seventh verses:

> Therefore let everyone who is godly pray to you [in other words, all
> those who are willing and ready to confess their transgressions]
>   while you may be found;
> surely when the mighty waters rise,
>   they will not reach him.
> You are my hiding place;
>   you will protect me from trouble
>   and surround me with songs of deliverance.

We've already talked about the fact that there is power in prayer—it works. And there is a special power in the prayer of confession.

You might think of it as the means by which you get plugged into God's power. Unconfessed sin can be like a short in an electric cord. You plug the cord into the wall and nothing happens. Something's wrong and the connection just isn't there. However, once you've found the problem, it's a fairly easy matter to fix it. Then you can plug in the cord and the power will flow through it. Sins short-circuit your connection to God.

Give your sins up to him. He is ready and willing to bless you right now! You can be close to God again. You can discover for yourself the joy of living in peace and freedom with God! You, too, can be surrounded with songs of deliverance. You can be declared *not guilty*. You can be seen by God as an example of righteousness and holiness, and you can begin to reach out to others in God's name.

7

God Blesses Those Who Reach Out to Others

The shooting took place during the middle of the afternoon on a crowded city street. The gunman had made no attempt to hide or disguise his identity. He merely walked up, calmly and coolly, and pumped three bullets into his victim, leaving him critically injured.

There were dozens of witnesses. There had to be. And yet, even though they were on the scene within minutes, the police couldn't find one single person who admitted to having seen what happened. Some said they had heard the gunshots. Others reported a commotion. But somehow, nobody had managed to get a look at the man who fired the gun.

As the police officers talked with people in the neighborhood, they became more and more certain that some of these people had gotten a very good look at the gunman. But nobody would give them a description. Why? Because nobody

81

wanted to get involved. Nobody cared enough about the victim to help bring the killer to justice.

In another part of town, an old woman died, all alone in her home. By the time somebody became worried and called the police, she had already been dead for several days, perhaps even as long as a week. When the police entered her home, they found a terrible mess: newspapers stacked almost up to the ceiling, trash spilling out of closets and drawers, roaches and other bugs all over the place, and the accumulated dirt and dust from years of neglect on the walls, floors, and furniture. The elderly woman had been living on social security benefits, which had barely been enough to pay her rent. Apparently, for the past several months of her life, she had occasionally resorted to eating dog food to keep herself alive. At least that's the way it looked because there were several cans of Alpo sitting on her kitchen counter, and there was no dog.

None of her neighbors knew the old woman had lived like that. Only one or two of them even knew her name. Nobody knew where she was from, whether she had a family, or what her life had been about even though she had lived in that house for as long as any of them could remember. You see, nobody cared enough to get involved.

And then there is the tragic case of Kitty Genovese. She walked along a street in her New York neighborhood, was accosted and stabbed more than thirty times while her neighbors turned off their lights and pulled their shades instead of running to her rescue. Nobody lifted a finger to help her. Her deranged attacker stabbed her again and again, leaving her lying on the sidewalk where she slowly bled to death.

Were those people in New York worse than the rest of us because they didn't want to get involved? Hardly. We are all very much the same. People haven't changed very much in the past two thousand years.

God's Commands Have Blessings Attached

Remember the parable of the good Samaritan? It was Jesus' story about a man who was traveling on the road to Jericho and was suddenly attacked by thieves. Not only did they steal his money, they beat him savagely and left him for dead. He lay battered, bruised, and unconscious on the side of the road.

As he lay there, two pillars of the Jewish community happened upon the scene—a priest and a Levite. These were men of God, and if anyone could be expected to show pity on this unfortunate stranger, they were the ones. Do you remember what they did? Those fine upstanding men crossed to the other side of the road so they wouldn't be expected to help the poor fellow. They didn't even want to look at him much less help him.

Then a Samaritan came upon the assault victim. Now the Jews of Jesus' day hated the Samaritans with a passion. They considered them half-breeds and heretics and didn't want anything to do with them. In fact, if a proper Jew was on a journey that would take him on a direct path through Samaria, he would often go hours out of the way rather than contaminate himself by passing through the territory that belonged to these despised people.

Yet in Jesus' story the Samaritan was the only one who had the compassion of God within him. Christ tells us:

> When he saw him, he took pity on him. He went to him and bandaged his wounds, pouring on oil and wine. Then he put the man on his own donkey, took him to an inn and took care of him. The next day he took out two silver coins and gave them to the innkeeper. "Look after him," he said, "and when I return, I will reimburse you for any extra expense you may have."
>
> Luke 10:33–35

And that wasn't the end of the story:

> "Which of these three do you think was a neighbor to the man who fell into the hands of robbers?" Jesus asked.

> ## *God will bless you right now if you, in turn, are willing to reach out to others and bless them.*

The expert in the law replied, "The one who had mercy on him."
Jesus told him, "Go and do likewise."

verses 36–37

Here Christ gives us the command to look after those who have been injured by this world. God will bless you right now if you, in turn, are willing to reach out to others and bless them. In the first two verses of the forty-first Psalm, we read:

> Blessed is he who has regard for the weak;
>   the LORD delivers him in times of trouble.
> The LORD will protect him and preserve his life;
>   he will bless him in the land
>   and not surrender him to the desire of his foes.
> The LORD will sustain him on his sickbed
>   and restore him from his bed of illness.

In the King James Version of the Bible, the word *weak* in the above passage is translated as poor. Both translations are accurate, because the point is that the Lord wants us to reach out to those who are having a difficult time in life and he promises that he will bless us when we do. In Deuteronomy 15:11, God even goes so far as to say, "I *command* you to be openhanded toward . . . the poor and needy" (italics mine).

What are the blessings that come to those who do reach out?

1. They will be delivered in times of trouble.
2. They will be protected and preserved in the land.
3. They will not be surrendered to the desire of their foes.
4. They will be sustained on their sickbeds and restored from the bed of illness.

This sounds like a pretty fair arrangement to me. It also gives us an easy choice with regard to investing our time and money. We can put all our money in the bank and draw interest on it, or we can invest some of it in helping the poor and weak thus receiving interest in the form of God's deliverance, protection, and sustenance.

Sometimes, however, God's blessings are not immediately apparent. An acquaintance told me about an incident that happened when he was on a long trip by car. He took a wrong turn, got lost, and pulled off the road to look at his map. After getting his bearings, the man prepared to pull back out on the road. At the last minute, for no real reason, he hesitated. As he did, a huge tractor-trailer rig barreled by. He hadn't seen the truck at all. Had he pulled out in front of it, he most certainly would have been killed instantly. What made him stop? Some people would say it was a coincidence. But I know this man and the compassion he has for the poor and needy; he'd give you his last dollar if you needed it. I am convinced that God was protecting his life.

God Calls You to Action

While reading the Book of Psalms during the writing of this book, I was struck by the fact that so many of God's blessings are pronounced on people who are taking action: walking in God's presence, meditating on God's laws, reaching out to the poor, helping those who are oppressed. God is a God of action, and he expects us to be a people of action.

Jesus was a man of action. Read through the New Testament and you'll find out how aggressive Jesus was when it came to ministering to people. While people often sought him out, hoping to receive a touch or an opportunity to hear the wisdom that came from his lips, the Lord also went to them so he could help them. At the synagogue, he told them that the kingdom of God was about to arrive in power and glory. During a funeral procession, he brought a poor widow's only son back from the dead, not because she asked him but because he was moved with compassion for her. When the Lord saw the money-changers polluting God's temple, he didn't stand back and shake his head and say, That's really too bad but there's nothing I can do about it. He went right after them, turning over their tables and driving them out of the temple with whips. Jesus was a man of action and he wants those who follow him to be the type of people who will go out into the darkness to attack and destroy evil things.

Of his church Jesus said "the gates of Hades will not overcome it" (Matt. 16:18). This gives us a picture of an aggressive, forward-moving army attacking the very gates of hell, knocking them down, and rescuing the people who have been enslaved by darkness and evil. God wants us to take action, to move forward, and he will bless us through it.

Not too long ago, a friend sent me the following thoughts. They remind me of those actions we can take—big and small—in order to bless others and receive God's blessings in return.

> Think freely. Practice patience. Smile often. Savor special moments. Live God's message. Make new friends. Rediscover old ones. Tell those you love that you do. Feel deeply. Forgive trouble. Forgive an enemy. Hope. Grow. Be crazy. Count your blessings. Observe miracles. Make them happen. Discard worry. Give. Give in. Trust enough to take. Pick some flowers. Share them. Give a promise. Look for rainbows. Gaze at stars. See beauty everywhere. Work hard. Be wise. Try to understand. Take time for people. Make time for yourself. Laugh

heartily. Spread joy. Take a chance. Reach out. Let someone in. Try something new. Slow down. Be soft sometimes. Believe in yourself. Believe in others. See a sunrise. Listen to rain. Reminisce. Cry when you need to. Trust life. Have faith. Enjoy wonder. Comfort a friend. Have good ideas. Make some mistakes. Learn from them. Trust others. Celebrate life.

But I Can't Do It by Myself!

Sometimes the problems in this world are overwhelming. They seem too big for one person to do anything about. Everywhere you look, even here in America, people are being affected by crime, poverty, sickness, loneliness, and bereavement. It can seem like we're swimming in an ocean of tears. And then we turn on the evening news to hear the latest horror from Bosnia or Rwanda or wherever it is that people have decided to slaughter and maim their neighbors and former friends. Like I said, sometimes the problems in this world just seem too big to face.

But God doesn't expect you and me to solve all of the world's problems. He simply expects us to make a difference wherever and however we can—one person at a time. Whenever we reach out to someone less fortunate, to one of the people that Scripture terms "the least of these," we are really reaching out to him.

In Matthew 25:34–40, Jesus puts it this way:

Then the King will say to those on his right, "Come, you who are blessed by my Father; take your inheritance, the kingdom prepared for you since the creation of the world. For I was hungry and you gave me something to eat, I was thirsty and you gave me something to drink, I was a stranger and you invited me in, I needed clothes and you clothed me, I was sick and you looked after me, I was in prison and you came to visit me."

Then the righteous will answer him, "Lord, when did we see you hungry and feed you, or thirsty and give you something to drink? When did we see you a stranger and invite you in, or needing clothes and clothe you? When did we see you sick or in prison and go to visit you?"

> The King will reply, "I tell you the truth, whatever you did for one
> of the *least of these* brothers of mine, you did for me" (italics mine).

Here, the Lord lists six ways in which we can reach out to others: We can feed the hungry, give water to the thirsty, give shelter to the homeless, provide clothing to those who are dressed in rags, give care to those who are ill, and visit those who are in prison. These things are simple enough.

Notice that the Lord didn't say: Put an end to world hunger, provide clean water for all the world's children, build shelters for every homeless person in the United States, and so on. He told us to do what we can, one step, one person at a time. And having done this, we must leave the rest up to him.

God Gave Us Each Other

You may remember that George Burns starred several years ago in a fun movie called *Oh, God!* He played God in the movie, making jokes about being the natural choice for the part since he and God were about the same age! Although there were some theological problems with the film—like most religious movies—it was fun and funny and had several good messages. One of these was that God has given us each other and he expects us to quit fighting and lying and cheating and to start treating each other with respect and kindness. This is true! He *has* given us each other to lean on, and he *does* expect us to treat each other as the brothers and sisters he has always intended us to be.

This is driven home by such Bible verses as Galatians 6:2: "Carry each other's burdens, and in this way you will fulfill the law of Christ."

A few years ago, I knew a man who had a particular need in his life. He was rather embarrassed about it and being somewhat proud, he really didn't want anyone to know he had this need. He prayed about it and hoped that God would just drop the answer out of the sky. The man didn't want anyone else to be brought into the picture.

But that's not what happened. Instead, some friends of his—caring people who also believed in God—found out about the need and pooled their resources to help him.

At first, he was embarrassed. He hadn't wanted others to know about his need in the first place, and he didn't like the idea of accepting what others had given him. This is fairly common—we human beings often find it easier to give than to take, because we perceive giving as an act of strength and receiving as an act of weakness. Everyone wants to be seen as strong. But the more my acquaintance thought about what had happened, the more he realized that God had chosen to answer his prayers through other people. This is almost always the way God works, largely because he wants us to see how much we need each other.

One of the laws of physics tells us that for every reaction, there is an equal and opposite reaction. This is true in the physical realm as well as the realm of the spirit. When we reach out a helping hand to others, we set into motion a chain reaction that will eventually come back to bless us. It may not be evident right away but it is happening nonetheless.

These blessings may come in a number of ways. You may experience financial rewards. You may be blessed with happiness and peace of mind. You may find that other people are drawn to you because of your giving attitude and that you are never lacking for supportive, caring friends. However the blessings come, I am confident that the moment you reach out, the events are set into motion that will bring blessings into your life.

The Bible says, "Cast your bread upon the waters, for after many days you will find it again" (Eccles. 11:1). In other words, you never lose what you give to others; it will come back to you in little serendipities.

Scripture also says, "Give, and it will be given to you. A good measure, pressed down, shaken together and running over, will be poured into your lap. For with the measure you use, it will be measured to you" (Luke 6:38).

It has been my experience that people who are blessed by God are active people. They are doing something. Rather than sitting around waiting for the blessings of God to come to them, they are busy touching others with God's kindness and love.

What can you do to reach out to the poor, the needy, and the weak? I don't know, but I'm sure you can do something! Whatever you do may seem small and insignificant to you, but God promises anyone who gives even a cup of cold water in his name will be rewarded and blessed because of it (see Matt. 10:42).

So look for ways to bless and know that you will be blessed because of it!

There Is a Refuge from the Storm

It was an ominous spring afternoon in the Texas panhandle, a land of small towns and huge farms, an area with some of the best farmland in the country, a place where the land stretches out flat in every direction as far as the eye can see. It had been one of those sticky, humid days that seem to be unnaturally calm.

Those who lived in this area—called Tornado Alley—could tell you this felt very much like the calm that comes before a storm. Sure enough, just before noon the first black clouds appeared in the eastern sky. They were small and seemingly insignificant, but as the day went on more and more appeared until the entire sky was filled. In the distance were occasional flashes of lightning and somewhere, probably over in Oklahoma, rain was pouring down.

The men and women working in the fields kept a wary eye on the eastern sky. So did the shoppers and the merchants in the nearby town. The storm seemed to be moving in their direction and, if a tornado was taking shape out there, well, they wanted to be ready. These people knew what a tornado could do. They knew it was one of the most powerful destructive forces in all of nature. They had seen tornadoes rip up everything in their path—trees, houses, barns, tractors, cars, trucks, people. They knew these storms could move with such terrific force they could take a single piece of hay or straw and drive it through a telephone pole. Just after four o'clock it became apparent that their worst fears were about to be realized. Some of the storm clouds had taken on a definite funnel shape.

In the small town, the siren began to scream out its warning. It was time to tie down everything that could be tied down, to get cattle and animals into their barns, and to get the heck out of the storm's way. Everyone knew where the storm cellars were and for miles around, men, women, and children headed as fast as they could for the nearest ones. Some of the children tightly clutched dogs, cats, and assorted other animal friends. A few of the women grabbed an heirloom or two, perhaps an album full of wedding photos. But there really wasn't much time to think about it. They had to get down in the cellars as quickly as possible. Once they were safe, they could pray that their houses would still be standing when they came back out again and the possessions they treasured most would not be scattered all the way to Amarillo.

The storm cellar on the Archers' farm was one of the biggest in the area. It could hold at least fifty people, and that's exactly how many people lived in the nearby neighborhood. It wasn't until all fifty were present and accounted for that the big wooden doors were pulled shut and the cross-bar slid into place to keep everyone secure against the force of the storm.

It turned pitch dark. For a moment it was deathly quiet. A small child began to cry, and this sent another baby into hysterics. The mothers did their best to hush their children and calm their fears. A man cursed and stomped his foot, saying that something had bitten him, maybe a spider; he hoped it wasn't a black widow. He didn't get much sympathy.

"Shhhhh!" someone said. "Listen."

They heard a rumbling noise in the distance, a muffled roar that sounded like the approach of a locomotive. But they knew this was no train. It was the tornado. As they listened, the sound grew in intensity. The storm was headed their way.

The rumbling grew louder and louder until it became an angry, deafening, awful roar. It seemed to be overhead. The big wooden doors creaked and groaned, moving up and down as the winds swirled over them at speeds of nearly 200 miles per hour.

It seemed, to the people in the cellar, that the storm went on for hours. Finally, after about fifteen minutes, it passed. The roar subsided into a low, distant rumble. It was time to come out and assess the damage. The crossbar was removed, and the big doors were pushed open. One at a time, the people emerged into the sunlight to an awesome sight.

It was easy to see the exact path the storm had followed as it headed west. Trees had vanished. Fences were gone. Shrubs had been uprooted. Cars had been overturned. Telephone poles had been toppled. Houses had been demolished. The tornado had left nothing behind.

If the winds hadn't been so devastating, the residents might have found the sight quite interesting. The zigzag path of the storm was very narrow. One tree was missing while another, fifty or seventy-five yards away, hadn't even lost a branch. One house would be a total wreck, while the house next door was sitting prim and proper with cushions still on the lawn furniture.

The damage, however, was extensive. It was clear that if that cellar had not been there—if the people had stayed at home and tried to ride the storm out—many would have been injured or killed. Even though property damage would run into the millions, not a single life was lost. Thankfully, everyone had been able to find a place of refuge during the storm, and so they all had survived.

In an average year, there are more than 500 tornadoes in the United States. If you've ever lived in the midwestern part of the United States, or if you live there now, I'm sure you know about these storms and the damage they can inflict. You realize that when a tornado is coming in your direction, you had better get out of its way. Hopefully, you know exactly where you will go and what you will do if one of those devilish winds should throw its fury at you.

In California, we don't know a lot about tornadoes. We get one every now and then, but their occurrence is rare. However, we do know quite a bit about earthquakes. And because they are so familiar to us, we usually don't let them stop us from going about our business. Many of us have developed a blasé attitude over the years. We tend to laugh at easterners who tell us they could never live in California because they'd be terrified that a major earthquake was going to hit.

However, those of us who live in Southern California, and particularly in the Los Angeles area, haven't been laughing so easily or so loudly since January 17, 1994. We were jolted out of our complacency and out of our beds when the big one hit just after 4:30 in the morning—4:31 to be exact. There was no sleeping through it. It was extremely frightening.

The shaking itself went on for less than thirty seconds, but those of us who lived through it know that it felt more like thirty minutes! Floors rocked up and down like those mechanical bulls popular during the late seventies. Walls swayed back and forth. Dishes and books clattered from cupboards and cases. And that was if you were lucky.

But a lot of people were not lucky. In the college community of Northridge, a three-story apartment building suddenly became two stories. The top two stories fell straight down, completely smashing all of the first floor apartments and the people who lived in them. Seventeen people died instantly in that one apartment complex. North of town, a motorcycle policeman was heading south toward Los Angeles and work. He had no way of knowing that the freeway just ahead had collapsed into the darkness and he died in the thirty-foot fall. There were many other fatalities that day. The destruction was enormous.

Where Do You Go When the Whole World Is Shaking?

Tornadoes are scary, but at least you can find refuge in a storm cellar. When a major earthquake hits, there is nowhere to go. The whole earth seems to be heaving in convulsions and there is no possible place of refuge—no escape from the terror. Yet even in a situation like this, those who understand the power and love of God know exactly where they can go. God is there waiting for them with open arms, saying, Come to me, and I will protect you.

Psalm 46:1–3 says:

> God is our refuge and strength,
>   an ever-present help in trouble.
> Therefore we will not fear, though the earth give way
>   and the mountains fall into the heart of the sea,
> though its waters roar and foam
>   and the mountains quake with their surging.

Remember the song that says "he's got the whole world in his hands"? Well, these words are true. As powerful as a tornado or an earthquake may be, there is nothing that comes close to matching the power of the One who created you and me and everything around us. If he is holding you safely in his hands, then there is nothing in the universe that can harm you. Earthquakes can rock and shake the world with all their might, but if God is protecting you, they won't even be strong enough to mess up your hair!

God is there offering refuge at all times, no matter what sort of calamity might be threatening you, whether a literal earth-

> *God is blessing you right now*
> *by offering you refuge*
> *in his arms, a safe harbor*
> *from the terrible*
> *storms of life.*

quake or tornado—or a storm of the spirit. After all, there are all types of storms that blow through a person's life: illness, loss of a loved one, job loss, financial reversal, difficulty in school, trouble in a marriage or friendship, problems with your children, difficulty with your boss. And while a tornado is terrible and an earthquake can be even worse, our emotional and spiritual storms can be far worse than any physical catastrophe life can throw at us. Yet through them all, God is there offering us a place of refuge, saying: "Come to me, all you who are weary and burdened, and I will give you rest. Take my yoke upon you and learn from me, for I am gentle and humble in heart, and you will find rest for your souls. For my yoke is easy and my burden is light" (Matt. 11:28–30).

As the psalmist writes: "Even though I walk through the valley of the shadow of death, I will fear no evil, for you are with me; your rod and your staff, they comfort me" (Ps. 23:4).

God is blessing you right now by offering you refuge in his arms, a safe harbor from the terrible storms of life.

One time Jesus and his disciples were in a small boat in the middle of the Sea of Galilee when a vicious storm blew up. As the wind howled, the waves began to sweep over the sides of the little boat. Frantically the disciples tried to keep the small craft afloat. In the middle of their panicked activity, they looked

around to find Jesus sleeping calmly through it all, as if nothing at all was going on!

"The disciples went and woke him, saying, 'Master, Master, we're going to drown!'

"He got up and rebuked the wind and the raging waters; the storm subsided, and all was calm. 'Where is your faith?' he asked his disciples" (Luke 8:24–25).

Was Jesus unaware that a storm was raging? Probably not. But it didn't really matter because he knew that in the midst of any storm he and his disciples were safe in the Father's hands. This is the way it is for you, too.

As I look around today, I see many people who are desperately in need of a place of refuge. I find individuals who are having trouble in their marriages or relationships. I come across families where children are involved with drugs or other illegal activities. I see young men and women who are getting sucked into gang violence, being forced to shoot and kill each other to prove their courage. They all need a place of refuge in an increasingly dangerous and violent time. The sad thing is that many of these people don't know that refuge is possible. They don't understand that God is always ready to provide shelter from the storms of life.

If I live to be 120 I will never forget the one time in my life when I desperately needed refuge, and God provided. It happened when I was on a boat in the middle of nowhere, halfway down the coast of the Baja peninsula. I was in the middle of an adventure that I had been planning for years (although I didn't expect things to be nearly as exciting as they turned out to be). The boat's steering gave out, in the middle of the night, 400 miles or so from the nearest port. If you know the Baja peninsula, you know that most of it is fairly rugged and isolated territory. In fact, there's only one place to get fuel between San Diego and Cabo San Lucas—a distance of about 800 miles. There aren't any harbors, either. There are some small islands you can hide behind if you're lucky enough to find one, but if

you're out on the open sea with the weather getting rough and you've lost your power to steer, there's not much left to do but pray.

And that's the position we were in. The sea was getting extremely rough. We were bouncing around like a ping-pong ball in a windstorm, and it was a very black night. Somehow, we were finally able to get some coverage from the heavy waters behind a small island but even here, the waves were much too rough for us to drop anchor. Besides, we could tell from our depth sounder that the water was 150 feet deep even though we were only a few yards from shore.

We didn't know what we were going to do. Then, off in the distance I thought I saw the glimmer of two lights—one red and one green. Anyone who's ever done any sailing can tell you that a red light next to a green light signals the entrance to a harbor. I rubbed my eyes, wondering if maybe I was seeing those welcome lights because I wanted to see them. But they were still there, shining through the darkness.

Because we had twin screws, we were able to manipulate the craft into a position to motor straight in the direction of those lights. As we drew closer, I blinked a couple of times, thinking that they'd probably be gone when I opened my eyes. But they were real, and they were marking the entrance to an honest-to-goodness uncharted harbor right out there in the middle of nowhere! In a few minutes, we were in a place where the water was calm and peaceful and where the light from the stars and moon reflected on the sea enough for us to see a little Mexican fishing village and drop our anchor. Exhausted and relieved, we drifted into a deep, peaceful sleep. We knew that in the morning, it would be a fairly simple matter to repair the steering and be on our way.

Now I've seen a lot of welcome sights in my life—my wife's beautiful face, the smiling faces of my children, a soft warm bed at the end of an exhausting day. But I'd have to say that those two lights rank right up there with the best things I've ever

seen. I honestly don't know what would have happened to us if that harbor hadn't been there. It would have been a fairly easy matter for the waves to throw us against the rocks or for the winds to carry us far out to sea. But God provided the harbor. I learned that night that there is nothing more comforting than coming into a place of pure refuge—a place where you don't have to worry about the weather or anything else that might make you uneasy.

Taste of the Lord

How do you find the refuge of the Lord? You simply turn to him and ask him to shelter you. Psalm 34:4–8 says:

> I sought the Lord, and he answered me;
>   he delivered me from all my fears.
> Those who look to him are radiant;
>   their faces are never covered with shame.
> This poor man called, and the Lord heard him;
>   he saved him out of all his troubles.
> The angel of the Lord encamps around those who fear him,
>   and he delivers them.
>
> Taste and see that the Lord is good;
>   blessed is the man who takes refuge in him.

I like this passage, and I find the part about tasting of the Lord especially intriguing.

Have you ever tried to get a child to eat something he doesn't like? If you're a parent, I'm sure you have. Maybe it was spinach or brussels sprouts or carrots.

"Come on, it's good for you!"

"But I don't want it."

"Just try it. You might like it."

"No I won't. I hate it! Yuck!"

Well, in this passage God himself is saying, Go ahead, taste me. See what I'm like. I promise you'll be pleased by the experience.

However, some people are stubborn. They're like little children with their arms crossed saying, No! I don't want a taste. I don't need God. I'll do it myself. They may have the idea that God is a stuffy being who speaks in "thees" and "thous" and who lives in a musty smelling building surrounded by stained glass and candles: If I ask God to help me, he might expect me to spend the entire rest of my life on my knees in a church somewhere!

God isn't limited to a church building or a Sunday morning worship service. Nor is he a sour old man sitting up in heaven keeping score of everything you've ever done wrong, waiting to punish you. He is the One who created everything you see—the mountains, the oceans, the flowers, the trees, the sunset, the rainbows, all the amazing beauty of the natural world. He is the One who put the trunk on the elephant and the majestic mane on the lion, and who painted the delicate wings of the butterfly. He is the One who invented laughter and came up with the concept of love. And, while I'm on the subject, let me mention (at the risk of offending some people) that he also invented sex. No, God is not some old fuddy duddy locked away in a cathedral hundreds of years old. The God who offers you refuge from the storms of life is alive and vibrant and exciting.

The old Alka Seltzer commercial said, "Try it. You'll like it." In the commercial, the guy did try something, he didn't like that something, and he wound up needing a long tall drink of Alka Seltzer. But "taste and see that the Lord is good"! God says, Try me. You'll like me. And he knows this is true. Once you've had the experience of tasting what it's like to be taken into God's arms for refuge, you'll never want to turn anywhere else.

The Importance of Trust

Trust is something that gets built up over time. For example, think about a father who is teaching his little girl to swim.

The first thing he wants to do is to help her become less afraid of the water. As he sets her on the side of the pool, he tells her to jump in and he'll catch her when she does.

"No, Daddy, I'm scared."

"Come on. I'll catch you!"

"Are you sure?"

"Yes, I'm sure."

"Do you promise?"

"Of course I promise."

"Well, okay. Here I come!"

The more that little girl trusts her daddy, the quicker she'll be ready to jump, and the further she'll jump, and before she knows it she'll be diving off the deep end and swimming the length of the pool.

It works that way with God, too. The first taste of his love and kindness lets us know we can trust him. And the more we taste, the more we are able to trust.

The last line of Psalm 34:8 says, "Blessed is the man who takes refuge [or trusts] in him." Once God gives you refuge in your first time of trouble, you will feel more secure. This is the blessing. When a second or third time of trouble comes along, you'll turn to him sooner and more confidently.

Look at Psalm 34:19. "A righteous man may have many troubles, but the LORD delivers him from them all."

Some people ask why the Lord allows trouble to come into the world. In recent years some teachers have taught that if we're living right, we won't have any trouble because God will protect us. But this is not what the Bible says. It tells us that if we're living, breathing, feeling, thinking human beings, then we're going to have times of trouble and difficulty on this planet. However, in the end, if we are looking to God for help, he *will* reach down and provide a way of escape. He *will* give us refuge.

You may be getting tossed around on the roughest of seas and you may think that the steering system in your personal boat is completely gone, but God won't let you be swept away. He won't let you be swamped and drowned. He will deliver you. In fact, whatever you are going through, he *is* delivering you right now.

False Gods

Sadly, there are many people who don't trust in God or turn to him for refuge. They turn instead to what I call false gods. These are:

1. self
2. money
3. things
4. other people

Let me explain why none of these will provide needed refuge.

Self

Have you ever seen a beautiful model on television doing a hair care commercial in which the model looks smugly into the camera and says, "Sure it costs more, but I'm worth it." How about the one where a woman pleads with other women, "Don't hate me because I'm beautiful." Well, as someone once said, "Any man who worships himself has a fool for a god."

Those who think their beauty or intelligence or athletic ability or business know-how is something they made for themselves are very mistaken. All of these things are gifts from God.

For more than one hundred years humanists have been saying that we can lift humanity out of the depths if we just turn to logic and self-awareness and leave the mythology of God and religion behind. In many ways mankind seems to be *re*gressing instead of *pro*gressing. Why? Because man does not have the power to take care of himself; he needs God's help and strength.

In the twelfth chapter of Luke, Jesus told a parable about a man who was terribly proud of all the things he'd done. This man had big barns and houses full of possessions. Yet these weren't big enough so he decided to pull everything down and rebuild on a grander scale. Once he had done this, he thought he'd sit back and take it easy for the rest of his life, thinking about how nice it was to have it made. Only he didn't have it made. That very night, God was going to call the man's soul into eternity. This man had left one very important factor out of his plans—God was in charge. He trusted in himself rather than God.

Money

There is no security in money; it can be wiped out overnight.

Every so often, the stock market behaves like a runaway roller coaster heading downhill. Each time this happens, millions of dollars are lost. So-called experts term this a "hiccup" and say that the market is readjusting itself. But it's a pretty severe hiccup that can wipe out the life savings of hundreds of small investors. What was a sure-fire investment yesterday can be a complete bust today, and even the safest investments may not be safe.

Here in California we've been "treated" to the trial of Lyle and Eric Menendez. The Menendez brothers are two young men who admitted to shooting their mother and father to death. They have been defending themselves by saying they were acting in self defense because they feared for their lives. Of course, in the process of killing their parents, they inherited a fortune worth more than twelve million dollars.

And they went through it in only a few years. In fact, the state of California is now paying for their attorney because the brothers could no longer afford to pay out of their own pockets. Their millions are gone. All that gold, obtained through such terrible circumstances, didn't make a particle of difference in the lives of those two brothers. If they are ultimately acquitted, they will be broke. If not, they will spend the rest of their lives in prison.

Money does not last. It is not a savior. But there's not a thing in the world wrong with having money. Poverty is not a blessing from heaven. Money is good in the hands of good people and bad in the hands of bad people. But money becomes a problem when you come to think of it as the most important thing in life and as the means for getting you through life without any problems. It can't. It won't. And it will let you down.

Things

In Southern California, we know about the way possessions let you down. We've seen huge, multi-million-dollar homes sliding down the hillsides and crashing in pieces into the valleys below. We've watched expensive homes go up in flames during the brush-fires that occasionally sweep across our portion of the "Golden State." We've seen a single fire or mudslide wipe out a lifetime's worth of possessions once obtained at great expense.

Anyone who tries to take refuge behind a pile of things is going to wind up bitterly disappointed.

Other People

Other people are not always going to let us down. You may have a good and loyal friend who stands by you your entire life. A friend like this is one of the greatest of life's treasures.

But people are people. We're flesh and blood creatures who are prone to making mistakes. We often let ourselves down, and we often let other people down, too.

When I was in college, I had a friend who wanted to date a particular girl on campus. He thought she was the most beautiful girl he had ever seen and if he could get a date with her, his life would be terrific. Not only did my friend get a date with her, he fell in love with her and married her. They came close to making it into *The Guiness Book of Records* as one of the shortest and unhappiest marriages on record. The marriage fell apart. For whatever reasons, my friend's relationship with her didn't make his life wonderful.

If you are looking for other people to save you from the storms of life, you're looking in the wrong place. The greatest people in the world are, after all is said and done, only people, and that means they are capable of failing you.

God, on the other hand, will *never* let you down. He will never turn his back on you. He'll never say one thing to your face and then turn around and say something else behind your back. He'll never tell you he's too busy to help you right now and ask you to give him a call later. He'll never come to you and say, I'm sorry, but I just don't love you anymore so I'm leaving. Unlike human love, God's love is all-consuming and does not change.

The Results

Alcoholics Anonymous maintains that a man will not give up his drink until he reaches the very bottom of the pit, comes to the point where he says he cannot go on, and starts grasping for something or someone to hold onto. In many ways, this is a basic lesson of life. People will keep on doing what they've been doing as long as everything is going their way. And then something happens that jolts them out of that reverie. Perhaps it's an illness, or a financial setback, or something as simple as the approach of their fortieth or fiftieth birthday. Whatever it is, suddenly, the person realizes there must be more to life, and he is finally forced to turn to God for help.

When I met Donna, my wife, she was a refuge for me. She would listen to me. She would give me good advice. She became a very good friend. Eventually I knew that I wanted to spend my life with her, and so I asked her to marry me. Our relationship is built on a growing, ever-deepening friendship. There is a feeling of refuge from the dangers of the world. At the same time, both of us know that our marriage is grounded in a relationship with Almighty God. As we have gone about the business of deepening our relationship with each other, we have also sought an ever-deepening relationship with him.

As you learn to turn to God on a regular basis, he will become closer and dearer to you. You will discover that those stormy winds aren't nearly as powerful or cold or frightening as they used to be. You will come to the point where your strength comes from the inner source of God's presence in your life. And you will know beyond the shadow of a doubt that you have the ability and the strength to cope with the disasters, struggles, and tasks of life in a way that you never before thought was possible.

Isaiah the prophet said it this way: "Those who hope in the Lord will renew their strength. They will soar on wings like eagles; they will run and not grow weary, they will walk and not be faint" (Isa. 40:31).

The great French thinker Voltaire once proclaimed that within one hundred years the Bible would have lost its meaning and become nothing more than a curious museum piece. Today, the Geneva Bible Society has its headquarters in his home. The power of God's Word will stand forever because God himself will stand forever.

This is the God who offers you refuge, right now. Turn to him. Take what he offers. This is his blessing for you!

9

Wherever You Are, God Is There with You

Richard Wurmbrand spent more than a dozen years in a Soviet prison camp because he refused to renounce his faith. Perhaps you've heard of him or read his book *Tortured for Christ*.

During his years of imprisonment, Reverend Wurmbrand was treated horribly. For years he was beaten on an almost daily basis. He nearly froze to death during the long harsh Soviet winters. He spent days, weeks, and months by himself, sitting in the lonely darkness of solitary confinement. The torture would have been enough to kill a strong man. The loneliness and boredom would have been enough to kill a lesser man.

But Reverend Wurmbrand knew a secret that sustained him during those terrible years. He knew that God was there in that prison cell with him, the same way he had been present thousands of years before when a man named Joseph was falsely accused and imprisoned in Egypt. (You can read about this in the Book of Genesis, chapters thirty-seven through fifty.)

Try as hard as they might, those Soviet prison guards just couldn't break this prisoner's spirit. Something was really strange about him. They were the ones who were free. They were the ones who ate hot meals every day. They were the ones who went home to their wives and children at the end of the day. Why, then, was this poor, miserable, mistreated, malnourished prisoner so content? Why did he sometimes seem downright happy? What did he have, in the poverty and loneliness of his jail cell, that they did not have in their lives?

What Richard Wurmbrand had was the joy of the presence of God. The Russians could take everything else away from him, but they couldn't strip him of his friendship with the Creator of the universe. In fact, Wurmbrand knew that even if they killed him, that wouldn't be enough to separate him from his Lord. He understood that physical death was but a door into another life—an eternal life with God. While he sat in the darkness of his prison cell, this man felt the sense of God's presence with him, and that presence gave him joy. As long as he knew God was with him, he could face whatever those prison guards threw at him—and he did.

> *Where God is*
> *there is excitement,*
> *there is peace,*
> *there is security.*
> *And more than anything else,*
> *there is joy.*

If God's presence brought joy to Richard Wurmbrand at such an utterly terrible time of his life, then I am completely confident that an understanding of God's presence will bring you and me the same sort of joy right now, at this very moment, regardless of anything else that may be happening. I can also say with complete confidence that God is willing to bless you right now with the joy of his presence. In fact, he *is* blessing you with the joy of his presence. All you have to do is open up your heart to him and receive this blessing. You see: Where God is there is excitement, there is peace, there is security. And more than anything else, there is joy.

Psalm 89:15 says, "Blessed are those who have learned to acclaim you, who walk in the light of your presence, O LORD. They rejoice in your name all day long."

Those who understand God rejoice in his presence; if they knew God was coming to town, they would run to meet him. But there are others who don't understand God, who think of him as stuffy and stodgy and even mean. These people would remain inside and keep their doors locked if they knew God was making a physical visit to their neighborhood.

Unfortunately, far too many people have grown up with the wrong image of God. They think of him as someone with a giant scorecard who delights in putting a mark against their names every time they do anything the least bit wrong, someone who likes nothing better than to throw thunderbolts and cause earthquakes and other natural disasters. No wonder we have organizations like Fundamentalists Anonymous, where people get together to overcome the fear of God put into them by their parents or other adults when they were small. Many of these people are guilty of throwing out God along with all the erroneous teachings about him they picked up as children. Instead of understanding that God really does exist but that what they learned about him was wrong, they come to think that everyone who believes in God thinks of him the same way that those who taught them thought of God. So they just won't believe in him at all. They believe their choice is either to believe in a score-keeping, mean-spirited God or no God at all, and they choose the latter.

But this is a far different picture of God from the one in the Bible. It tells us that God is love, that his loving-kindness is better than life. He is not willing that any should perish, but that all should have everlasting life. He is always ready to listen and ready to forgive our sins when we ask. That doesn't sound like an ogre to me.

When you hear the sound of God's "footsteps," you can rejoice because a friend is approaching. When you are in the presence of God, you can be at ease because you are in the presence of a friend, someone who loves you, who cares about you, and who comes to build you up with freedom, joy, and happiness.

Practice the Presence of God

Several years ago, Reverend Jesse Jackson formed an organization known as PUSH (People United to Save Humanity). One of the purposes of this organization was to raise the self-esteem of black and hispanic teenagers, to lift them out of the gang mentality often pervading the inner city, and to help them take their place as constructive contributing members of society. One of the things Jackson had people do was to stand up and shout as loudly as possible, "I *am* somebody! I *am* somebody!" He wanted them to say it until they believed it. And it worked!

If you say something loud enough and long enough, you're going to get to the point where you believe it. The reverse is true as well. If you constantly talk down to yourself with words like "I'm nobody" or "I'm useless," then you'll begin to believe them, too.

I'm telling you this because it is important for the believer to practice God's presence. I'm not suggesting that you stand in front of a mirror and punch your fist in the air and shout, God is with me right now! God is with me right now! I am not suggesting that you play mind games or that you engage in some sort of psychological fantasy. What I am saying is that you remind yourself of something that is very true—that God is with you right now. Thinking about it won't make it any more real than it already is. It simply helps awaken your heart to the reality.

Maybe you're lying in bed, reading a few pages in this book before you turn the light off and go to sleep. If that's where you are, God is blessing you with his presence right now. Perhaps you're in the lunchroom at work and you only have a few minutes before you need to get back to the tasks of the afternoon. If that's where you are, God is with you now, and he'll continue to be with you when you go back to your job, whatever it may be. Maybe you're sitting in your car waiting to pick up your kids from school or soaking in a bathtub full of bubble bath or sitting in your den on a quiet evening. Wherever you are, stop, take a minute, and think about the fact that God is blessing you with his presence right now!

Imagine you are sitting in your living room one night. Someone rings your doorbell. You get up from your favorite chair where you've been reading your afternoon newspaper and impatiently walk to the door. You figure this is probably a salesman or a neighborhood kid selling candy or raffle tickets. You open the door only to discover that Bill Clinton is standing on your front porch!

"Hi," he says. "I hope you don't mind. I just thought I'd stop by for awhile. Do you have a few minutes?"

What would you do? However you may feel about Mr. Clinton as president, I doubt that you would say, "Well look, Bill, I hate to be rude, but I was just starting to read Ann Landers' column. So if you don't mind, maybe you could come back another night when I'm not quite so busy." Instead, you would most likely be thrilled to have the president of the United States choosing to visit you in your home. It would be an honor to think that he valued you enough to want to talk to you and hear what you have to say about the state of the country.

Well, you know what? Bill Clinton probably won't ever come to your house. But God does! In fact, he is there already. And if you thought the president's gracing your home with his presence should make you feel excited, just think about the fact that the One who created everything you see around you is with you right now! When we understand this, we will have a perpetual sense of awe as well as a better understanding of the way he cares for us. And we will not be easily shaken.

One of the ways I am reminded of God's presence in my life is through reading the Book of Psalms. I'm often amazed by the similarity between my life experiences and feelings and those of David. And because you and I share living space on the same planet, I'm confident that my life experiences are very much like yours. It helps me to realize that God was with David when he was going through times of emotional turmoil, feeling defeated and alone and abandoned. It helps me to know that God stayed close to the king even when he was weak and sinful. It helps me to see how God ultimately carried David through those times of defeat, loneliness, and weakness and that David wound up shouting God's praises.

We spend time with God when we pray, meditate, and listen for his voice. Some people hear this and reply, Sure *you* do all those things. After all, you're a minister. People expect that of you. Where did we get the idea that prayer was something set aside for professional clergy? Prayer is for *everyone*, and it's a great way to get close to God.

Another avenue for practicing the presence of God is to keep a journal of your early morning conversations with God. You'll want to write down the things you pray about, keeping a list over time of the way your prayers are answered. You may even want to write down impressions and insights that come to you as you wait before God, things you believe have come from him. I know people who keep journals like this. In fact, I do it myself. It's always a terrific reminder of the fact that God is with me.

Before we move on, I want to turn to the little book, *The Practice of the Presence of God*, written by Brother Lawrence in the seventeenth century. In this book, Brother Lawrence explains how he came to have an understanding and sense of God's presence with him as he went through his day.

> Having found in many books different methods of going to God and divers practices of the spiritual life, I thought this would serve rather to puzzle me than facilitate what I sought after, which was nothing but how to become wholly God's. This made me resolve to give the all for the all; so after having given myself wholly to God, that He might take away my sin, I renounced, for the love of Him, everything that was not He, and I began to live as if there was none but He and I in the world. Sometimes I considered myself before Him as a poor criminal at the feet of his judge; at other times I beheld Him in my heart as my Father, as my God. I worshipped Him the oftenest that I could, keeping my mind in His holy presence, and recalling it as often as I found it wandered from Him. I found no small pain in this exercise, and yet I continued it, notwithstanding all the difficulties that occurred, without troubling or disquieting myself when my mind had wandered involuntarily. I made this my business as much all the day long as at the appointed times of prayer; for at all times, every hour, every minute, even in the height of my business, I drove away from my mind everything that was capable of interrupting my thought of God.
>
> Such has been my common practice ever since I entered in religion; and though I have done it very imperfectly, yet I have found great advantages by it. . . . It also begets in us a holy freedom, and, if I may so speak, a familiarity with God, wherewith we ask, and that successfully, the graces we stand in need of. In time, by often repeating these acts, they become habitual, and the presence of God rendered as it were natural to us.

Brother Lawrence continued:

> Let all our employment be to know God; the more one knows Him, the more one desires to know Him. And as knowledge is commonly

the measure of love, the deeper and more extensive our knowledge shall be, the greater will be our love; and if our love of God were great, we would love Him equally in pains and pleasures.

Just as we should love God whether we are experiencing pain or pleasure, he is with us equally at all times of life, whether things are going well or not, whether we are completely able to sense his presence or not. This is his blessing to us each and every day.

God Comforts with His Presence

A couple of years ago, I almost lost my father. He was fine one day; the next day he was injured and the doctors were telling us that his life was in danger. Even though I knew that my father's life was in God's hands and that God was there for our entire family, that was a terrible time for me. Thankfully, he recovered completely and today he is back doing what he loves to do—preaching from the pulpit of the Crystal Cathedral, overseeing the production of *The Hour of Power* telecast, and reminding people all over the world that God loves and cares for them.

Looking back on it now, I can see that God's presence was never so real to us as it was during that time we thought we might lose my father. God was there in an almost tangible way, loving us and helping us deal with the trauma and sadness of Dad's illness. I will never forget what happened when John Wimber, the founder of The Vineyard Ministries came to my father's bedside to pray for him. Reverend Wimber was attending a conference in Amsterdam when he heard about my father's hospitalization, and he and his wife came quickly to give their love and support. We gathered around the bedside, and, as my father lay there, deep in a coma with monitors and machines hooked up to various parts of his body, Reverend Wimber prepared to pray.

But then a very interesting thing happened. He stood there with hands stretched out over my father and his eyes tightly closed in an attitude of prayer, but he never said a word. We just stood there for a minute or so and then, without a word of prayer being uttered, walked out of the intensive care unit.

Once we were outside, Reverend Wimber told me, "I'm sorry I didn't say anything. It's just that I have never felt such a presence of God over one man before. There must be untold millions of people praying for him. Standing in that wonderful aura I could find no words."

I can't imagine what it would have been like if we had had to pass through that difficult time alone. What a comfort it was to be able to feel God's care and concern in such a strong way. And isn't this just like God, to enter our lives in a fuller, deeper way when we are passing through a time of trial or sorrow.

In the middle of this period, during the time the doctors still weren't certain my father was going to survive, the *National Enquirer* asked me to write a short article about my reaction to the situation. They even gave me the title for it: "Why I Know My Father Is Going to Make It." Here is an excerpt from that article.

In spite of what happens, I know my father is going to make it. There is always the possibility that he may not physically survive. He is in intensive care. It is a miracle that he is still alive today. I could make a long list of probable ifs, any of which could have taken his life already. Life is but a vapor. It is so easily lost and gone. Any perfectly healthy, loving, positive person can be enjoying life today and be gone tomorrow.

In spite of this, I know my father is going to make it, because he has a friend who is dearer than I, a friend who doesn't leave his side at night . . . a friend who doesn't sleep . . . doesn't take meal breaks, who doesn't leave him even for a moment. His name is Jesus Christ.

My father has an advantage in life that many people have not had. He has given that same advantage to me. He started walking with his friend Jesus at an early age. He put his hand in His hand when he was a boy. His life has been with him ever since. Still is. Jesus took his life as a boy and gave it back to us to enjoy him and his creativity . . . his humor and his smile and his intensity and his glare, his drive and his enthusiasm, his love and his touch. What this experience has done for me is remind me that Dad's life, as we know it, will not last forever—only a lifetime. He may grace us for a minute or a score, but I know that he will make it, because he is already there. Life everlasting does not begin at physical death, but begins the moment you take the hand of Jesus and say, "I want you to be my friend, too." He will take your life as it is today and give it back to you in a new and a beautiful way, full of peace, expanding in love, and growing with faith. This has been the goal of my father's life—putting the hand of his best friend Jesus Christ in the hands of others.

Let me tell you a story I heard a few weeks ago. (I can't vouch for this story's authenticity, but I don't have any reason to doubt the veracity of those involved.) A woman who was barely old enough to be a grandmother died of cancer in a hospital with her immediate family gathered around her bed. She was a godly woman who died in peace, with the assurance she was going straight home to be with God.

The family had prayed and prayed right up until the moment of her death that something miraculous would happen and that she would be restored to health. No one was ready to let her go. But at the moment her spirit left her body, they felt a comforting and loving presence enter the hospital room. Feelings of love and peace swept over them. It wasn't as if a life was dying but more like a life was being born. They knew, instinctively, that God had come to take their mother, sister, and wife to his bosom. They not only sensed his compassion for their sorrow but also his reassurance that this separation was only temporary and that reunion lay ahead.

Nobody said anything. Each one was too awestruck. Only later did they all agree that every one of them had felt it.

Later that day while taking care of the paperwork and other things that had to be done at the hospital, some members of the family inadvertently overheard a hushed conversation between two nurses. "The woman who died in room 435 must have really been a godly person," the first one remarked.

"Why do you say that?" the other nurse asked.

"Just go in that room," came the reply. "There's something sacred in there. It's like a church or something. You can feel it as soon as you walk through the door."

I don't know what you think about this but I think those people got a small taste of what it's like to be in the presence of God.

You'll Want to Shout Hallelujah

The last book in the Bible is the Revelation of John, written by the apostle John after he had been exiled to the island of Patmos for his crimes against the emperor (the chief of which was his refusal to renounce Christ). In this book, John writes about a vision he had of heaven. Specifically, he wrote about multitudes of people from every nation who were praising God together.

> After this I looked and there before me was a great multitude that no one could count, from every nation, tribe, people and language, standing before the throne and in front of the Lamb. They were wearing white robes and were holding palm branches in their hands. And they cried out in a loud voice: "Salvation belongs to our God, who sits on the throne, and to the Lamb."
>
> Revelation 7:9–10

How does this sound to you? Wearing a white robe and holding a palm branch in your hand and crying out praises to God. Chances are it doesn't sound like the way you'd like to spend eternity. Like most people, you probably read a passage of Scripture like this and hope there's something more exciting than that to do in heaven.

We may not understand it, but it's going to be exciting to stand directly in God's presence. I am convinced that the feeling is going to be so thrilling that we will have to shout,

"Hallelujah!" Being directly in God's presence is going to be the highest high anyone could ever feel, the exhilaration above all feelings of exhilaration.

If you are an athlete, you know the thrill of engaging in a fierce competition and coming out victorious. Being in God's presence is going to be better than that. If you are a parent, you remember the thrill that came over you the first time you saw your newborn baby. Being in God's presence is going to be more thrilling than that. If you're married, you probably remember the excitement you felt on your wedding day. Being in God's presence is going to be more exciting than that. It will be greater than it was for Neil Armstrong the first time he stepped on the moon, for Sir Edmund Hillary when he finally reached the summit of Mount Everest, and for Christopher Columbus when he first spotted land after more than two months at sea.

If you want to know the excitement of being in God's presence, turn to the seventh chapter of 2 Chronicles, where Solomon was dedicating the temple he had built for the worship of God:

> When Solomon finished praying, fire came down from heaven and consumed the burnt offering and the sacrifices, and the glory of the LORD filled the temple. The priests could not enter the temple of the LORD because the glory of the LORD filled it.
>
> 2 Chronicles 7:1–2

The presence of God was so strong that the priests couldn't even enter into the temple where he was!

There are a number of other references in the Old Testament to the power of the presence of God. In fact, the Bible tells us that no mortal man could look directly into the face of God because the experience would prove fatal. That was the unbelievable power and glory that emanated from God's presence.

I'm sure you get the picture. In this life, we don't often get a very full sense of God's presence. Yet, every now and then he does give us a small taste of what it's like to be near him, and that in itself can be overwhelming. What does it take to know his presence? It takes opening up your heart to him and asking him to open the eyes of your spirit so you can sense his presence.

In the fourteenth chapter of John, Jesus tells us that anyone who loves the Father and who strives to obey his teachings can know he is with them in a special way: "My Father will love him, and we will come to him and make our home with him" (v. 23). God won't make his home with habitual liars, or those who cheat and steal and commit adultery. But this doesn't mean you have to be perfect before God will reveal his presence to you. It simply means that you must be willing to *try* to live the kind of life he wants you to live. After all, God knows that none of us is perfect, and he is always ready and willing to forgive us when we fall short of perfection.

God Will Take Your Hand

What does it mean to have God in your life? It means he's there, right there in your house with you. He's watching over you when you sleep. He's there to greet you when you first open your eyes in the morning. He's there at the breakfast table when you're reading your morning newspaper and eating your bowl of Wheaties. God is there with you when you're lonely and when you have a house full of friends. He's there when the tears are rolling down your face or when you're laughing so hard that your sides hurt.

In short, he is always there. What you and I have to do is learn to practice being in his presence. We have to remind ourselves constantly that God is right there with us wherever we are, whatever we may be doing. I don't mean to imply that God is some big cosmic snoop who never gives you a moment of privacy. Don't think of him as someone always looking over your shoulder, checking on you to see what you're up to. He is there to comfort, support, and protect you when you need him, and, whether you realize it or not, you always need him.

Wherever you want to go in life, as long as it is in keeping with God's desires for his people, he is willing to take your hand and walk with you. When he does, be assured that your final destination will be the right one, even if it doesn't turn out to be the destination you originally had in mind.

When my father was a young man, God offered his hand to him and my father started walking with God. He was only five years old when my Great Uncle Henry, who was ninety-three, ruffled his hair and said, "Robert, I think you're going to be a minister when you grow up." From that point, my father knew exactly what he was going to do. As he went through school, he always had in mind that the pastorate was his destination. He went on to Hope College in Holland, Michigan, and then to Western Theological Seminary. From there, he took over the pastorate of a small church in the town of Ivanhoe, a sub-urb of Chicago. All the time, he knew that God was leading him and that he was exactly where God wanted him to be. When the call came to move to California to start a church in Orange County, he knew that God's hand was in that too and that he was supposed to go.

The only problem was there wasn't a church building, just an old drive-in theater. And so my dad would stand up on the top of the snack bar and preach to people who sat in their cars. He couldn't even see their faces. He didn't know how they were responding to his sermons. He had no idea if they were even listening. For five years he preached that way, standing on top of the snack bar every Sunday, until finally his congrega-tion was able to build a church where people could come in and sit in the pews and he could actually see their faces and get to know them as their pastor.

Today that church is the Crystal Cathedral, which I believe to be one of the most beautiful and impressive structures in California, if not in all of North America. I believe that building, dedicated to the glory of God, serves as a wonderful reminder of God's loving faithfulness. It is not a monument to the successful preaching of Robert H. Schuller (although I have to admit that, as his son, I think my dad is a dynamic preacher), but it stands as a testimony to the faithfulness of God. That church is a physical testimony to the fact that God will take our hands and lead us into his blessings if we'll let him. My father is going about the business that he knew God was calling him to, in a place where he can help others take hold of God's hand as well.

I hope and pray that this book will at least leave you with the understanding that you too can walk with God through life. And when God has you in the palm of his hand, he will not let you go.

> Fear not, for I have redeemed you;
>   I have summoned you by name; you are mine.
> When you pass through the waters,
>   I will be with you;
> and when you pass through the rivers,
>   they will not sweep over you.
> When you walk through the fire,
>   you will not be burned;
>   the flames will not set you ablaze.
> For I am the Lord, your God,
>   the Holy One of Israel, your Savior.
>   Isaiah 43:1–3

I hope you understand more clearly than ever before that God is with you right now, wherever you are. If you listen, you can hear his voice. Don't be afraid of its sound. Put your hand in his. Walk with him and go where he leads. He will always be with you, for as he promises, "Surely I am with you always, to the very end of the age" (Matt. 28:20).

I want to conclude this chapter with a prayer. I hope that you will make these words your own.

O Lord, I love you. I hear your joyful sound, the sound of your foot-steps walking with me. I know you are with me, walking beside me, holding my hand. Thank you, Lord, for your abundant love. Thank you for your freeing grace. Please take my burdens away and make me new. Help me to sense your presence in everything I do, everywhere I go. And help me to live each moment knowing that you are with me. Help me to walk, O Lord, with you. Amen.

10

God Wants
to Instruct You

I've heard it said that adversity makes some people better but makes others bitter.

I've seen enough to know that's very true.

I've also heard it said that experience is the best teacher—that you can learn quite a bit from going to "the school of hard knocks." I'm convinced of the painful reality of both of these statements. There is much to be learned from passing through difficult times.

I'm not saying that God is allowing you to be bruised and battered just because he wants to teach you something. But at the same time, if you *are* being bruised and battered by the world, God can use those difficult experiences to teach you some very important things.

He can teach you about your own strengths and weaknesses. He can teach you humility. Or trust. Or how you can help others. Or any of dozens of other things.

The important thing to remember is that God is always ready and willing to teach you—to give you the benefit of his all-encompassing wisdom and knowledge.

Have you ever had a teacher who revolutionized your life? Perhaps you were like me, sort of drifting along in school, doing what you needed to do to get by, and then a teacher came along that fired your imagination and got you excited and serious about learning. Maybe it was a teacher who made history come alive for you in a new way, or an English teacher who opened your eyes to the pleasure and the thrill of reading great literature or putting your deepest thoughts down on paper. Or it could have been that man or woman who suddenly made sense out of all those mumbo-jumbo geometric and algebraic equations that always seemed like gibberish before.

God is far superior to those teachers. Can you imagine what it would be like if he were coming to your local community college as a guest lecturer? I wonder how many people would sign up to take the course? How many people would want to learn from the wisdom of the One who created the entire universe? I have a feeling the answer is in the thousands, and they would come from all over the world.

Perhaps you are familiar with Gary Larson's "Far Side" cartoons. One of my favorites has God appearing on the television show *Jeopardy*. God sits there, as small children might picture him, with a long flowing white beard. His opponent looks at him with a mixture of awe and annoyance while the show

God knows it all, and he is willing to share his knowledge with you!

host says, "That's right! God wins again." Larson's drawing shows the score at something like 40,000 for God and zero for his opponent. If God did make an appearance on a game show, none of the other contestants would stand a chance. There's nothing God doesn't know!

When Albert Einstein came out with $E = mc^2$, he was only discovering what God already knew eons ago. When Wilbur and Orville Wright discovered the power of flight, they were merely putting into practice principles God had built into the universe when he first designed it. When Archimedes got so excited that he shouted, "Eureka! I have found it!", he hadn't come up with any knowledge that was hidden from God. God knows it all, and he is willing to share his knowledge with you!

God knows everything! He has all knowledge, all wisdom, all the great secrets of history. He understands the solutions to all the great mysteries and controversies that have raged for ages. And he wants to be your teacher! How could anyone refuse an offer like that!

Psalm 94:12 says, "Blessed is the man you *discipline*, O LORD, the man you teach from your law; you grant him relief from days of trouble" (italics mine).

Discipline is involved in any kind of learning. This is true of the wisdom that comes from God as well. It's not something he is going to drop into the minds of those who don't want it or care to pursue it. But he will never turn away from those who diligently apply themselves to learning from him and about him. As James, the brother of Jesus writes, "If any of you lacks wisdom, he should ask God, who gives generously to all without finding fault, and it will be given to him" (James 1:5).

Godly Wisdom Never Changes

If you have children in school, then you know how quickly things change in this world of ours. The things that I was learning as fact just twenty years ago are no longer considered true. For example, the field of science is growing by leaps and bounds. Even Einstein's theories on space and time are being challenged these days. And when it comes to geography, forget it. Almost every country on the African continent has changed its name over the last twenty years. In the past five years, several independent countries have sprung up from the one Soviet Union. For a while it seemed that boundaries were changing on an almost daily basis, and it's not over yet.

Scientific knowledge changes. Geography changes. Political systems change.

But Godly wisdom never changes. He knows everything *about* everything, but the wisdom that God most wants to share with you has to do with eternity, the shaping of the human soul. He wants to teach you how to live in such a way that you will be blessed and will bless others.

Godly wisdom teaches us that "a man reaps what he sows" (Gal. 6:7). That was true five thousand years ago, and it will be true five thousand years from now. Godly wisdom tells us that "A man's pride brings him low, but a man of lowly spirit gains honor" (Prov. 29:23). That, too, will be true throughout eternity. And godly wisdom tells us that it is by grace that we are saved, "not by works, so that no one can boast" (Eph. 2:8–9). Again, the wisdom that God gives will be of use to you throughout eternity!

Let me ask you a question. Where did you learn the things you know? Was it through practical experience? Or did you merely take as fact what somebody else told you? Did you read it in a book and then try it to find out whether it worked? For example, your kindergarten teacher taught you the simple truth that $2 + 2 = 4$. You found out that was true then, and it's still true today. If you had two apples and Farmer Gray gave you two more apples, you would have four apples. That's not subject to debate. But there are other kinds of truths that are. For example, I grew up thinking of milk as some sort of super formula, like Popeye with his spinach: If you drank enough milk there wasn't anything you couldn't do. In my case, the love of milk went deep because my mother and father were both raised on dairy farms and my uncles are big milk producers, even to this day.

In my younger days I was probably one of the top milk drinkers in the country. I didn't drink it by the pint, quart, or even the gallon. I put it away by the barrel! I'd start off my day with a couple of glasses of milk in the morning. When I went through the cafeteria line at school, I'd get three of those little pint-sized cardboard cartons. After school or sports, the first thing I'd do was pour myself another couple of glasses. Following that, I would have another few at dinner and then two more before bedtime.

I'm sure you've seen the commercial on television that says, "Milk does a body good." It shows some small skinny guy growing into a Mr. America type. Well, I drank so much milk that I should be out right now palling around with Arnold Schwarzenegger! However, I developed a horrible case of cystic acne over my entire body and especially on my back. It was very painful and, although I tried almost everything to get rid of it, nothing worked. It caused me so much pain that I could not sit comfortably in a chair.

One day while getting my hair cut, my barber said, "You know, Robert, I bet if you'd stop drinking milk, that would solve your problem."

Quit drinking milk? But milk does a body good, doesn't it? It certainly couldn't be the source of anything harmful. Besides that, I had been going to a dermatologist for several months, and if he couldn't solve the problem, what made this barber think he could? Still, the acne hurt so bad I was willing to try anything. So I quit drinking milk. And guess what, the barber was right! The acne went away in a matter of weeks.

It's not my intention to bad-mouth milk, but this experience taught me an important lesson. I found out that in spite of everything I had previously learned, drinking large quantities of milk wasn't good for me. Some of my knowledge was wrong.

Sometimes the "knowledge" we acquire is bad, and sometimes it's so confusing we don't know what to believe. For example, experts used to tell us that eggs were loaded with cholesterol and should be avoided at all costs. Now they say it's perfectly fine to eat as many as four eggs a week. They used to tell us that beta carotene helped to prevent cancer. Now they're not sure. Not too long ago I saw recipes in two different magazines designed for health conscious people. What one recipe suggested as a common part of the daily diet, the other said we should completely avoid. There are facts and then there are facts!

What Did *You* Learn in Kindergarten?

A few years ago, a man named Robert Fulgham wrote a fascinating little book called *All I Ever Need to Know I Learned in Kindergarten.* It was a simple yet inspiring book, beautifully written. The title came from an essay in which the author reminded us of some of the important things we learned when we were tiny children—things like sharing, taking turns, being nice to other people, and so on. Very true, isn't it? When I look around at what goes on in the adult world today, I often think of how nice it would be if we could live up to all those important things we learned in kindergarten.

Not long after this book came out, Donna and I visited our daughter's kindergarten class on a back-to-school night. We met her teacher, a woman who has been teaching kindergarten for more than twenty years. I'm not sure what I was expecting. I suppose that when I thought of someone who had been dealing with a room full of boisterous five- and six-year-olds for more than twenty years, I expected her to look tired and haggard, perhaps with her eyes bulging out of her head and her hands shaking. I was surprised to find instead that this woman was young and pretty. Not only that but her room was neat as a pin. I knew right away that she had to have some special secrets. So I sat on a little chair and waited for her to reveal them.

"You know," she said, "one of the things we do around here is that we make the children do everything. We have rules, and we expect everyone to follow them."

The first rule was that the kids were not allowed to say, "I can't." She explained that the very first day of school would be absolute bedlam. The children wouldn't know how to do anything, and they would run around whining and crying, saying, "I can't! I can't!" Out comes Rule Number One. From that point on, even if a student thought he or she couldn't do something, the student had to say, "I'll try." And then the child had to give it the good old kindergarten try. Surprise! When the kids really started trying, they would discover they could do a lot more than they originally thought they could.

The kids in that teacher's class were going to learn something about life. For one thing, they would learn not to believe the lie that says you can't do it. Instead, they would find out they shouldn't say "can't" until they had given it a try. I knew this would help them tremendously as they went through life. They might master the most complex theories of physics or calculus, but none of it would be as important as those basic truths they learned from this wise kindergarten teacher.

That's the way God wants to deal with us. He wants to teach us foundational truths that will keep us in good stead for the rest of our lives. But this brings up an important question, namely, how does God teach us?

Looking for Answers in the Bible

The usual answer to this question is that God teaches us through the Bible. Although I believe this is true, I also believe it's a bit simplistic to let it go at that. The Bible is a deeply complex book and not easily understood by everyone. If this wasn't true, we wouldn't have so many different denominations—we wouldn't quarrel over such subjects as the importance of the sacraments, whether infants or adults should be baptized, and whether or not the Book of Revelation should be taken literally or allegorically.

However, while the finest, brightest minds in the world have struggled with some of the contents of the Bible, within its pages are verses of Scripture that ring as loud and true and real as life itself. It is not essential that we all understand these passages exactly alike. When judgment day comes, God is not going to give us a pass or fail test. But in order to overcome these problems, it's best to have a foundation for your study, a written plan that will guide you in a structured way through the book. It's also good to study the Bible within the context of a group, led by someone who has devoted himself to studying and understanding the book. Only remember as you study that many of the truths in the Bible are indisputable while other portions are open to varying interpretations.

The Lord wants to instruct us through his Word. It contains great truths regarding the origin of the universe, God's love for mankind, the life that awaits us beyond this one, the way God expects us to live in this life, and so on. For example, the thirteenth chapter of the Book of 1 Corinthians tells us God's definition of true love:

> If I speak in the tongues of men and of angels, but have not love, I am only a resounding gong or a clanging cymbal. If I have the gift of prophecy and can fathom all mysteries and all knowledge, and if I have a faith that can move mountains, but have not love, I am nothing. If I give all I possess to the poor and surrender my body to the flames, but have not love, I gain nothing.
>
> Love is patient, love is kind. It does not envy, it does not boast, it is not proud. It is not rude, it is not self-seeking, it is not easily angered, it keeps no record of wrongs. Love does not delight in evil but rejoices with the truth. It always protects, always trusts, always hopes, always

perseveres. . . . And now these three remain: faith, hope and love. But the greatest of these is love.

1 Corinthians 13:1–7, 13

In this one passage, God holds up a mirror by which we can judge our own actions. Naturally, in my position as the pastor of a church, I have done quite a bit of marriage counseling. I'm convinced that if every married couple would take the words we've just read to heart and try to live up to them, there would be very little strife in our marriages.

The Bible has a great deal to teach us about the way we live.

The Development of a Proper Thought Life

Finally, brothers, whatever is true, whatever is noble, whatever is right, whatever is pure, whatever is lovely, whatever is admirable—if anything is excellent or praiseworthy—think about such things.

Philippians 4:8

Proper Relationships with Others

Love your neighbor as yourself.

Matthew 22:39

Our Relationship with God

If we confess our sins, he is faithful and just and will forgive us our sins and purify us from all unrighteousness.

1 John 1:9

Anyone who trusts in him will never be put to shame. For . . . the same Lord is Lord of all and richly blesses all who call on him, for, "Everyone who calls on the name of the Lord will be saved."

Romans 10:11–13

Any appliance you buy comes with a handbook, a set of instructions that tell you how to assemble, operate, and keep the item in good working order. I have heard the Bible described as the "Manufacturer's Handbook." Because God is the "manufacturer" of this world and everything in it— including you and me—it's a good idea to read his instruction manual.

I've also heard the Bible referred to as a love letter from God to humankind. I think this is a good description, too. There are many references in this book to God's constant care for his people. It holds many promises regarding God's love and faithfulness. Once a person comes to understand that God really does love and care for him, there will be very little in life that can shake him.

At the risk of offending some people, I need to say at this point that I am opposed to what I call "Bible worship." Let me explain. Some people put the Bible on the throne, considering it to be the source of all wisdom. It isn't. Instead, the Bible is a book that *points* to the source of all wisdom—the One who does belong on the throne, God himself. So, the first way God is blessing us through his instruction is that he has given us the Bible. This brings us to the second way God wants to bless us, and that is through our right to talk to him directly.

God Instructs Us through Prayer

My father once wrote a book called *Life's Not Fair, But God Is Good*. In it, he had this to say about prayer:

> When life's not fair which way do we turn? Try prayer. Prayer is a universal practice. The human being is, by nature, a spiritual being. We all yearn to reach out with our souls. We all attempt to transcend our humanity through prayer. The human being was created in the image of God. We are, therefore, innately, instinctively, incurably spiritual. Even those who have no exposure to religious philosophy or doctrine or teaching whatever, still feel the natural impulse within the breast which calls them to communicate with their Creator.

When life doesn't seem fair, when things aren't going the way they're supposed to go, we can go to God and know that he cares enough to listen . . . and not only to listen but also to give peace and wisdom to know how to handle the difficulties that come our way.

Am I saying that God is going to speak to you in an audible voice and tell you exactly what to do? He could (although he has never spoken to me this way). But there is something that happens when we spend time communicating with him. There is a strength that comes from sitting and waiting in his presence. There are insights that come—insights that, I'm convinced, will come directly from God's heart to yours.

It's the wise man or woman who understands that God is the source of all knowledge and wisdom. Because of this, because he is also a loving father and friend, it doesn't make sense not to pray.

Now, please don't think I'm saying that prayer is the source of wisdom. It's not, God is. But prayer *is* the means by which we can gain access to his wisdom.

Perhaps you remember the story of Moses' encounter with God in the form of a burning bush. When Moses asked God what his Name was, God replied, "I AM" (Exod. 3:14). This is the reality of God's presence that is instilled within the human psyche. We are all born with the deep-seated knowledge that God does exist—that he is. When we try to deny this reality, we find ourselves swimming against the tide of humanity. To deny the existence of a Supreme Being goes against the natural tendency of the human spirit.

People of every society pray, instinctively. They may not know for sure to whom they are praying, but they pray nonetheless. They know somebody is out there listening to them, whether they call him "Great Spirit" or "Jehovah" or any other name.

If you stop and wait and listen for God, he will come and put his hand in yours. You will hear him whispering to you: *You're going through some tough times right now, aren't you? I'm here now. Hold on, and I'll carry you through.*

Prayer can be the key to unlocking a tremendous healing force in yourself and in others. I've seen it happen time after time. I've seen people healed by prayer: some physically, some spiritually, some emotionally. As a pastor I have prayed with thousands of people—the rich, the poor, the devout, the unbelieving. Prayer has always brought about positive results. Sometimes those results were dramatic; sometimes they were not so dramatic. But people are always touched and lives are always changed in some way when prayer is brought into the situation.

Unfortunately, some people think of prayer as a quick way to get what they want from God. They come to him like children going to Santa Claus with a Christmas list: Give me this, give me that. This is not the type of prayer I'm talking about. I'm referring to that prayer that seeks to develop a relationship with God and that asks him for strength and wisdom.

The Bible says, "Perseverance must finish its work so that you may be mature and complete, not lacking anything" (James 1:4).

Patience and prayer go hand-in-hand. Day by day, as you continue in prayer, you will begin to see the solutions to your problems. You will see circumstances beginning to line up to give you a way out of impossible situations. You will begin to experience peace in the midst of turmoil. Day by day, the bruise on your arm will begin to dissipate. The bumps, the sores, the gashes that have been imposed on your soul by the simple process of living in this often difficult world will begin to disappear. If you keep your life and your heart open to his will, he will pull you through. He will teach and instruct you, and your life will be measurably better because of it. Alfred Lord Tennyson was absolutely correct when he wrote "More things are wrought by prayer than this world dreams of."

There is power and wisdom and instruction in prayer. When my father almost died, a few years ago, he was in the Netherlands and experienced a severe brain hemorrhage. He was rushed to the hospital, and for several hours his life hung in the balance.

A few weeks following his emergency brain surgery, I received a letter from a neurosurgeon, Dr. David Spindle, who visited my father in Amsterdam when he was in the hospital. The doctor wrote me that he was totally amazed when he saw the recovery my father was making. What astounded him was that my father hadn't asked any questions about his surgery or health, but instead reached out, grabbed the doctor's hand, and prayed for him, for his well-being, his travels, his family, and his health.

Dr. Spindle is a man who has been involved in literally thousands of brain surgeries. He knows what such a surgery can do to an individual. He understands that it takes weeks, and sometimes even months, even to begin to recover. Yet, my father was strong and so full of concern, not for himself but for someone else. This doctor learned something by the experience.

I believe that my dad's miraculous recovery is proof of the power of prayer, but there's more to the story. A few months before his illness, one of our *Hour of Power* employees—a man named Yope Post who runs our office in Europe—was in Amsterdam. He was on his way to the airport to leave town when terrible chest pains nearly doubled him over. He knew he was having a heart attack, so he asked to be taken to the nearest hospital.

The doctors couldn't figure out what was wrong with him. Because they were totally baffled, they sent him to another larger hospital across town. The doctors there couldn't figure out what was wrong with him either, so they referred him to a third hospital, which in turn sent him to Free University Hospital. There they ran an exhaustive battery of tests and let him know that, even though the pain he was experiencing was severe, it was not life-threatening.

Yope Post was with my dad in Amsterdam when he suffered his cerebral hemorrhage. He insisted that my father be taken immediately to Free University Hospital, even though it was quite a distance from my dad's hotel. Mr. Post didn't want my father shuttled from hospital to hospital to hospital but to go directly to the place where he could immediately get the treatment he needed. Without the insistence of his friend, my dad would have been taken to the nearest place where emergency treatment was available and shuttled through the system. Had that happened, he would have had permanent brain damage and might even have died.

Mr. Post had to argue with the ambulance driver. "He has to be taken to Free University Hospital," he insisted.

"I'm not allowed to do that. I have to take him to the nearest hospital." That hospital was only five minutes away from the hotel.

"I don't care what you're allowed to do or what it takes!" Mr. Post directed. "He's going to Free University."

The driver had no choice but to give in. As it turns out, Free University Hospital is the only place in the city of Amsterdam where my father was able to receive the treatment he needed. When he arrived, he was in a coma and his condition was critical. There was not another hospital within a radius of one hundred miles where the surgeries that saved his life could have been performed.

I believe that Yope Post experienced those terrible chest pains so my father's life could be spared. God fits all the puzzle pieces of life together for the good of his people. All things do work together for the good of those who love God. He can even bring good out of the bad if we'll let him. What's more, I know that God was answering the prayers of all the wonderful people who pray for my father's health and safety.

Don't ever discount the power of prayer. There is an old saying, "Pray as if everything depends on God but work as if everything depends on you." I like this saying, but I believe the emphasis should be on the first part of the sentence. Pray as if everything depends on God because it does!

When Jesus preached his famous Sermon on the Mount, one of the things he said was, "Blessed are the meek, for they will inherit the earth" (Matt. 5:5). People sometimes have a difficult time understanding this particular beatitude, because they don't understand the meaning of the word 'meek.' They think it means a little mouse of a person who is afraid of his own shadow. But that's not what Jesus is talking about. He is referring to those who are willing to wait patiently upon God, allowing him to instruct, guide, and shape them into what he wants them to be. In the end, these people will triumph over all the evil and sorrow the world can throw at them. They will inherit the earth.

God Instructs through Good Friends

A third way God wants to bless you right now with his instruction is through the counsel of wise friends and acquaintances.

If you don't know some people whose wisdom you trust and value, then I suggest you start looking for them. They're all around you—in church or school, in your place of business or your social organization. They're there if you'll just look for them.

Once you've found these people, you have to be willing to ask for their advice when you need it. And then you must consider it carefully after it has been given. In other words, decide that you're not going to reject or accept advice merely on the basis of whether you agree with it. I've known people who seek advice from dozens of people until they finally find someone who agrees with them, who tells them to go ahead and do what they want to do in the first place. Anyone with this attitude is only wasting the time of those whose advice and instruction he seeks. (It's apparent in a counseling situation as well, when people don't really want your counsel but merely want you to give your blessing to whatever it is they're doing.)

God doesn't always tell us what we want to hear. He tells us the truth. People who are listening to him won't always tell us what we want to hear either. They may say some things that are hard to accept and maybe even painful. But pain is not always an enemy; it can be a source of growth and strength, as any athlete will tell you. One person who will tell you the truth, even at the risk of hurting you, is worth much more than one hundred friends who always pat you on the back and agree with you no matter what (make that *four hundred* friends!).

The Bible has a story about a king who surrounded himself with four hundred such friends and who failed to listen when someone who could have helped him told him the truth. This is found in the eighteenth chapter of the Book of 2 Chronicles. It concerns a prophet named Micaiah and a couple of kings named Jehoshaphat and Ahab.

Ahab was planning to go to battle against a neighboring nation, and he wanted Jehoshaphat to commit some of his soldiers to the effort. For his part, Jehoshaphat was agreeable to the plan, but first he wanted to make sure the Lord was on their side. Ahab thought this was a fairly reasonable request, so he called in a number of his prophets—four hundred to be exact—and asked them whether God would give them the victory.

The prophets came in before the two kings, but you can bet they weren't about to give any bad news. In those days, it was true that the bearer of bad tidings was often killed for his efforts. The prophets agreed that, yes, it was a perfect time for the kings to go to battle, that God would give them a mighty victory, and that they'd be back home in no time, sipping champagne and swapping war stories.

For some reason, though, King Jehoshaphat didn't feel comfortable with what these men were saying. Wasn't there just one other prophet they could ask, someone a bit more stable than these wild-eyed fellows, someone who was obviously more intent on listening to God than in pleasing the king?

Ahab said there was one other prophet. "But I hate him because he never prophesies anything good about me," he bemoaned.

Jehoshaphat insisted on hearing what this man, named Micaiah, had to say. Ahab must have been terribly annoyed by this, but he needed Jehoshaphat's help and so he went along. The king sent his messengers to bring Micaiah so he could prophesy concerning the great battle that was about to be waged.

When the messengers got to Micaiah, they told him, "All the other prophets are telling the king he's going to win a great victory. If you know what's good for you, you'll tell him the same thing."

Micaiah just looked at them and sighed. "I can only tell them what God tells *me*!"

This lone prophet stood before the two mighty kings, both of whom were anxious to hear of the victory that was about to be theirs. God spoke to him and told him that they would not only lose the battle but that, if they went to fight, King Ahab would be killed.

That wasn't what the kings wanted to hear, and Micaiah knew it. Still, he had to tell them what the Lord had said. (It wasn't what the other prophets wanted to hear either. In fact, one of them came up and slapped Micaiah on the face for making such a terrible prophecy!)

The prophecy made Ahab mad. The king of Israel commanded his guards, "Take Micaiah and send him back to Amon the ruler of the city and to Joash the king's son, and say, 'This is what the king says: Put this fellow in prison and give him nothing but bread and water until I return safely.'

"Micaiah declared, 'If you ever return safely, the LORD has not spoken through me'" (2 Chron. 18:25–27).

The kings should have listened to him but they didn't, not even Jehoshaphat who had been the one to insist on hearing Micaiah in the first place. They marched off to war. They didn't have to do it; God had given them fair warning. They could have decided to wait until a better time to fight.

The battle turned out just the way Micaiah had prophesied. It was a terrible disaster, with the combined armies of Israel and Judah suffering a crushing defeat. Ahab was killed when an enemy soldier shot his arrow at random, and it lodged between the sections of the king's armor.

How many men and women have failed because they have done exactly what Ahab did? How many others have surrounded themselves with those who only told them what they wanted to hear? How many kingdoms have been lost, how many companies have gone down the drain, how many relationships have been destroyed because of people who insisted on surrounding themselves with "yes" men? Ahab and Jehoshaphat certainly have plenty of sad company.

I remember reading something similar about Louis XVI, the king who was overthrown by the French Revolution and beheaded with his queen, Marie Antoinette. Because the king had surrounded himself with men who insisted on telling him how popular he was and how much the common people loved him, he had no true idea of the depth of the wrath that burned against him, until it was too late for him to escape with his life.

God's instruction may not always be what you want to hear; nevertheless, it is always for your benefit. It is always something that will help you. God may warn you that you are headed down a wrong path. When he does, it is because he is giving you time to change directions. He may advise you to stop engaging in some behavior that is harmful to you. It's not because he doesn't want you to have any fun, but because he loves you and wants you to be safe and well. He may tell you not to do something that you've always wanted to do because he knows it would lead to personal disaster.

On the other hand, the Lord may tell you exactly what you want to hear. He may say, Go ahead with this thing you want to do; it will bring you blessings and great joy. He may tell you,

You're on the right path, and I'm pleased with you. Or he may simply instruct you in ways that are neither immediately good or bad but which are important for you to know as you make your way through life.

The point here is that we need friends we can trust, who believe in God and in living for him, and who want to help us as we live for him.

If you don't have any friends like this right now, look around and see if you can find someone who will agree to serve as a counselor or mentor to you. Maybe there's someone in your church, an older man or woman, who would agree to take you under his or her wing and give you some of the benefit of their years of experience. Maybe it's someone who is not older than you but who has demonstrated wisdom, credibility, and faithfulness—someone you trust to tell you the truth, who would be willing to share on a deeper level with you.

If you know such a person, you may want to start the relationship by asking him or her to lunch or dinner so you can get to know each other. If the things you're learning about this person verify what you've always believed, you can ask if he would be willing to serve as your mentor, to get together with you every once in a while to talk about what's going on in your life, give you the benefit of his wisdom, and seek God in your behalf.

Having someone you can share with, confide in, and trust to tell you the truth at all times can be a tremendous blessing. Remember: *nobody* is above needing the instruction of God that can come through the loving counsel of a good friend. I know that God is willing to bless you right now by giving you his instruction through such a friend.

The Bible tells us that King David was a man after God's own heart. He wrote dozens of beautiful psalms in which he clearly and passionately expressed the loving relationship he knew with God. You can't get much closer to God than David was. And yet when David fell into the sin of adultery, and then compounded it by having his lover's husband murdered, the humble prophet Nathan had to go to him and confront him regarding what he had done (see 2 Samuel 12).

Since David was a powerful man, the king of the entire nation, he could have had Nathan put to death with the snap of his fingers. But David knew that Nathan was right. He realized that the prophet was speaking words that came from the heart of God, and he was willing to listen to anything God had to say. As close as David was to the Lord, God still used another man as the means for carrying his instructions. May we all be so wise!

Most of us are very short-sighted. We only see the temporary struggles, aggravations, and disappointments. On the other hand, God is very long-sighted. He sees all of eternity. I've heard it said that when God looks at your life, it's like he is picking up a roll of movie film and stretching it out and seeing everything at the same time. In other words, he sees every frame all at once. You and I, because of our limiting vantage point, can see only one small frame at a time.

I think this is a pretty good description of the way it really is. God sees every action in context of the whole. He knows what the results of each step or mis-step will be, and he knows how he is going to work things out so that the big picture comes together as a blessing.

Everywhere you look these days, you find those three-dimensional, hidden-picture paintings. When you first look at them they look like some abstract design, but if you keep looking, pretty soon you see a three-dimensional picture of a familiar object. It may be the Statue of Liberty or a group of dolphins leaping in the surf or even the cross. All of a sudden the picture seems so plain you don't know why you didn't see it in the first place.

This is often the way God works in our lives. We're so close we can't see the big picture. It looks like many meaningless squiggles to us. Sometimes it doesn't really make any sense at all. But then, all of a sudden, there it is and we wonder how we could have missed it before.

We need to have an eternal perspective. We must pray that God will help us to see things the way he does. When we come to that point, it will be a lot easier to take temporary setbacks in stride and to pay attention to the Lord's instructions when he tells us to do something we really don't want to do or not to do something we really do want to do. You see, whatever is going on in your life, if you're trusting God and looking to him as your helper and guide, he is blessing you.

Don't ever forget that God may be blessing you by saying no. For example, an acquaintance of mine was looking to buy an expensive house in a newly developed area. The houses were beautifully landscaped, the yards were spacious, and the entire area was in a picturesque setting. He desperately wanted to buy a particular house but for a variety of reasons couldn't make the deal. He kept trying to work things out, but everywhere he turned there seemed to be another obstacle in the way. Finally it became apparent that he just wasn't going to get the house, so he let it go and tried to put it out of his mind.

A couple of years later he happened to be in the area and decided to drive by and look at his dream house. He wanted to see how the people who lived there were taking care of it. There was a big surprise waiting for him at the development. It turned out that those expensive homes had been built in a flood plain, and some of them were literally sinking into the ground. Some owners were having to spend thousands of dollars to jack their houses up out of the muck, to plug up sinkholes with fill-dirt, and to shore up the foundations of their houses. What had looked like a paradise had turned into a nightmare. For the first time, he bowed his head and said, "Thank you, God, for not letting me get that house." God's no had been a blessing rather than a curse.

Sometimes it is fairly easy to see why God says no. In my friend's case it only took a couple of years to discover the reason. Sometimes it's much harder to see why God doesn't agree and give us what we want or think we need so terribly. We may not get the answers to some of our questions until we reach the other side. For now, all we can do is trust God and know that he always has our best interests at heart.

Don't ever forget that God is blessing you right now by giving you his instruction. He will do this through his book, the Bible, through prayer, and through the counsel of godly friends.

11

You—Yes, You— Have the Right to Wear God's Name

Back in chapter 3 we discussed the story of David and Goliath when we talked about the fact that it is perfectly all right to give to God in order to bring his blessings into your life.

You may remember that we talked about how Goliath, a giant of a man nearly nine feet tall, had issued a challenge to the entire Israelite army. He would fight the Israelites' strongest, bravest man in a face-to-face, winner-take-all battle. If he won, then the Israelites must surrender to the Philistines. But if, on the other hand, an Israeli man was able to defeat Goliath—and from the looks of it, there wasn't much of a chance of that happening—the Philistines would surrender.

I want to take just a moment to get back to that long-ago battlefield, to imagine how Goliath must have felt when he saw the skinny shepherd boy coming out to meet him in hand-to-hand combat.

I'm sure he must have thrown back his head and roared with laughter. Certainly, Goliath expected that anyone who would accept his challenge would be a champion—someone strong and rugged, someone armed with his own spear, javelin, and coat of armor, someone who could fight him on an almost equal footing. He didn't expect the only taker to his challenge to be a young boy who looked more like he belonged on a playground than a battlefield.

> Then Saul dressed David in his own tunic. He put a coat of armor on him and a bronze helmet on his head. David fastened on his sword over the tunic and tried walking around, because he was not used to them.
>
> "I cannot go in these," he said to Saul, "because I am not used to them." So he took them off. Then he took his staff in his hand, chose five smooth stones from the stream, put them in the pouch of his shepherd's bag and, with his sling in his hand, approached the Philistine.
>
> Meanwhile, the Philistine, with his shield bearer in front of him, kept coming closer to David. He looked David over and saw that he was only a boy, ruddy and handsome, and he despised him. He said to David, "Am I a dog, that you come at me with sticks?" And the Philistine cursed David by his gods. "Come here," he said, "and I'll give your flesh to the birds of the air and the beasts of the field!"
>
> David said to the Philistine, "You come against me with sword and spear and javelin, but *I come against you in the name of the LORD Almighty, the God of the armies of Israel, whom you have defied.*
>
> 1 Samuel 17:38–45

You know what happened next. David put one of those stones in his sling, whirled it around his head, and then let it fly. It found its mark, hitting Goliath in the forehead and causing him to fall to the ground. As quickly as he could, David ran over, pulled Goliath's huge sword from its sheath, and killed him.

David was able to do what he did because he understood something very important: There is nothing else on earth as powerful as the name of God.

One thing that's very important to understand here is that David was not invoking the name of someone he didn't know. He had an intimate relationship with God. He wasn't invoking God's name as some sort of magical charm. There is a story in the New Testament, in the nineteenth chapter of Acts to be exact, about what happened to some men who tried to use God's name when they had no right to do so. When they tried to bring healing to a demon-possessed man "in the name of Jesus whom Paul preaches," the demonized man said that he knew Jesus, and he knew Paul, but he didn't know them. Then he leaped on them and beat them up! (Acts 19:13–16).

But David was part of God's family. He was saying, I am a child of God's and because of that I have the right to use his name!

God gives you and me the same right: to be part of his family and to use his name—and there is no greater name than the name of God.

The Name *Does* Matter!

Psalm 118:26 says, "Blessed is he who comes in the name of the LORD." Are you a son or daughter of God? Then you always come in the name of the Lord, and you are always blessed.

As the Old Testament Book of Isaiah says, "You will be called by a new name that the mouth of the LORD will bestow" (Isa. 62:2). In the New Testament Book of Revelation, we read, "Him who overcomes I will make a pillar in the temple of my God. Never again will he leave it. I will write on him the name of my God and the name of the city of my God, the new Jerusalem, which is coming down out of heaven from my God; and I will also write on him my new name" (Rev. 3:12).

This doesn't mean that your life will be one long party with one good thing piled on top of another. But it does mean that God will always be with you, loving and comforting you even in times of tragedy or distress.

When I buy something with a credit card or use my driver's license for identification to write a check, I'm often asked whether I'm related to my father.

"Are you your father's son?"

My reaction is always to wonder who else's son I could possibly be.

"Are you related to Robert Schuller?"

"I *am* Robert Schuller," I say, pointing to the name on the driver's license or credit card.

"No, I mean are you related to Reverend Robert Schuller, the minister?"

"I *am* Reverend Robert Schuller, the minister."

"No, I mean the guy up at the cathedral."

Once we get the matter straightened out, I'm always happy and proud to tell them that yes, I am related to the guy up at the cathedral. No doubt about it, I'm proud to be my father's son.

How about you? Are you proud of your family name, of the heritage your father and mother have brought you? Unfortunately, many people would answer no to this question.

A while ago I was visiting in the home of a friend who traces his ancestry to Scotland. Hanging over his fireplace was his family crest, a sword and shield combination dating back hundreds of years. As I was admiring it, he started to tell me what each symbol meant, how old it was, and how he had been involved in the process of tracing his family's history. He talked about it with great enthusiasm and more than a little bit of pride. I don't blame him. I think it's wonderful to be able to know something about one's family history—about the name that has been handed down through several generations.

That's one reason I always want to think twice before I do anything that might smudge the Schuller name in the least. I'm proud of that name, and I want my kids to be proud of it, too. My forefathers have taken good care of it; they've treated it with respect and done their best to keep it bright and shiny.

Rick Nelson once recorded a song titled "Legacy," in which he sang, "All that I leave I bequeath to my son . . . and ask his forgiveness for all that I've done with his name."

I don't know about you, but I don't ever want to be in the place of having to apologize to any of my children for anything I've done with their name. That's not to say that I don't make mistakes. We're all human, after all. But I will do my best to honor my heritage, because a name that you can really be proud of is one of life's great treasures. You can leave a lot of wonderful things to your children when you die, but a good name is very near the top of the list. If you are a father, I hope you feel the same.

Yet, in spite of this there is one name that is better, stronger, and more powerful than any family name on earth—the name of God. If you belong to God's family, then you have the right to wear his name as a son or daughter of the Almighty. God allows you to wear the name of the One who created the entire universe. Isn't that an exciting thought?

One of the Ten Commandments is that we are not to take the name of the Lord our God in vain. What does this mean? When I was a child I thought that it meant using the name of God, or Jesus, for a swear word. I think this is partly true. (It really bothers me when I hear people use the name of Christ as an epithet. Someone hits his thumb with a hammer, and the first words out of his mouth are Jesus Christ! My immediate reaction is to want to say, Do you know him, too?)

But there is a deeper meaning to this commandment and thus a much greater error committed by those who violate it in this deeper way. If you ask God to take you into his family, then you take a pledge to live a Christian lifestyle to the best of your ability. The person who goes to church on Sunday and prays like his soul is on fire to show everyone what a good, religious person is like, but who goes back to the business world on Monday and starts cheating and lying—that man has taken the name of the Lord in vain and violated the third commandment.

In today's society, we don't think very much about the meaning of a name. Parents often give their children names that are popular or sound nice. When I was growing up in the sixties, for example, I don't remember knowing a boy named Jason, and there weren't many girls named Jennifer. Then both of those names became "in," and suddenly the world was full of Jasons and Jennifers. It's interesting to see how things change. What was popular yesterday may not be so popular today, and what is popular today may not be popular tomorrow.

The names we give our children today are not chosen the same way names were selected in Bible times. *The Bible Almanac* explains:

> Names were very important in the world of the Old Testament. Each Hebrew name had a meaning, and it became an important part of the infant's life. Jewish people believed that they must first know a person's name before they could know the person himself. . . . Therefore, the act of choosing a name for an infant was a serious responsibility. . . .
>
> Often the name referred to a personality trait that the parents hoped would describe the child as he reached adulthood. Names like Shobek ("Preeminent") and Azan ("Strong") can best be understood in this light.
>
> pages 445–46

Names are important to God. For example, Genesis 17:5 tells us that God changed Abram's name to Abraham. Why? Because Abram meant "exalted father," but Abraham meant "father of nations." This new name reflected the promise God gave to Abraham that he would be the father of not only one nation, but a multitude of nations. In this same passage, the Lord also changed Sarai's name to Sarah (v. 15), which meant "princess." In Genesis 32:28, Jacob wrestled with God, and the Lord changed his name to Israel, meaning "one who has power with God."

You see, names are important to God. This is why he is willing to give you a new name, and not only a new name, but *his* name!

Think for a moment about the power that resides in a name. Have you ever heard it said that it's not so much *what* you know, but rather *who?*

Several years ago when my daughter was just a baby, I lived in Santa Ana and had to commute ten miles every day to the Crystal Cathedral, which is in the city of Garden Grove. Depending upon where you live, ten miles may or may not be a great distance. In the Los Angeles/Orange County area, it can be quite a journey through bumper-to-bumper traffic, especially when you're in a hurry. (Ask anyone in Southern California how far away some place is, and they'll almost always answer you in minutes rather than miles!)

On this particular day I was in a hurry because I needed to take a bottle to our baby, Angie. Angie's mother had called me from the cathedral and asked me please to bring it to her when I came in at noon. I was running late and fully aware that babies can get awfully cranky when they're hungry and there is no milk. So, admittedly, I was driving faster than I should have been.

I hadn't made it very far down the freeway when I looked in my rearview mirror to see something that made my heart sink: flashing red lights. The lights were for me, so at my first opportunity I pulled over, stopped, and waited for the officer to come up and give me the inevitable ticket.

As he approached, I rolled my window down.

"Good afternoon," he said, "may I see your driver's license and registration?"

I already had them ready for him. "Yes, sir."

He looked at my driver's license. "Robert Schuller," he said. "Are you any relation to that guy at the cathedral?"

I nodded. "He's my father."

Instead of pulling out his book of citations, the officer handed the license and registration back to me.

"Well, you have a nice day," he smiled. "But take it a little bit slower, okay?"

He didn't have to tell me twice! I drove off carefully, thankful that I had such "powerful" connections.

This is the way it is for you. No force in all of nature can defeat you when you are a friend of God, and not only a friend but in fact a relative. Do you think that any force in the world can defeat you as long as you are standing there covered by God's name? No way!

Using the right name can open doors for you. A man wanted to help his son get into a particular prestigious university. The boy's grades were very good, but they weren't outstanding enough to assure his admission. While waiting for a business meeting one day, the father struck up a conversation with a gentleman he had just met. During the conversation, his son's desire to attend this college came up.

"Why, that's my school," the man said. "Graduated from there in 1962. In fact, I'm on the board of directors for the alumni committee." The man pulled his business card out of his wallet. "Here's my card. You call the admissions office, give them my name, and who knows? Maybe it'll do some good."

The man was being modest. It did a lot of good. Doors were opened, and the young man was admitted into the university.

I heard it said that we are only six people away from knowing everyone in the world. You (1) know someone who (2) knows someone who (3) knows someone who (4) knows someone who (5) knows someone who (6) knows Gorbachev or Bill Clinton or George Bush or another prominent figure.

Let's go the other way. My father knows Gorbachev. I know my father. Therefore, I am two people away from Gorbachev. If you know my father, you are only two people away from Gorbachev. If you don't know my father but know me, you are three people away from Gorbachev. If you don't know me but know someone who does, you are four people away. If you don't know someone who knows me, but know someone who knows someone who does, then you're five people away. And finally, if you know someone who knows someone who knows someone who knows me, then you are the maximum six people away from Gorbachev!

While it sounds fantastic, researchers tell us that this is the truth, that we are only six people away from any other person, and this means we are only six people away from the most powerful men and women in the world.

But—and this is even more exciting—you are *not* six people away from God. The all-powerful Ruler of the Universe knows you personally, by name, and he gives you the privilege of being involved in a one-to-one personal relationship with him.

When you were a kid at school did you ever get picked on? That's probably a dumb question, isn't it? Everyone got picked on at some time or another. There have always been bullies, beginning in the days of Cain and Abel, and, unfortunately, I'm sure there always will be. (When Socrates was a little boy, some tough kid was probably stealing his lunch money and threatening to punch him in the nose after class!)

If you were lucky, you had a big brother or sister who loved you and who was willing to stand up for you. Wasn't it fun to watch the terror come into that bully's eyes when he realized you had a bigger sibling who was ready to pound him into the ground, just the way he had threatened to do to you?

"You mean you're related to him?"

"That's right. So, do you still want me to hand over my milk money?"

Well, God is on your side. And because he is, it doesn't matter in the least who or what is against you!

If you belong to God's family you have the right to use his name. There is incredible value in the name of God, and he is willing to give that value to you.

A few years ago, a couple in suburban Milwaukee invited an art appraiser to come to their home to look at a painting which they thought might be of value. They were wrong about that particular painting. However, while the appraiser was in their home, he noticed another painting hanging on the wall. The couple hadn't treated this second painting with much respect, even though it was beautiful, because they figured it was a reproduction of a work by Vincent Van Gogh and probably hung on walls in houses all over the country.

The appraiser wasn't so sure. The detail seemed too rich and expressive to be a copy. In order to be completely certain, he took a closer look. This look only verified his first impression. The painting was a Van Gogh original. Imagine how excited that couple was when they found out the painting that had been hanging on their wall for years was worth all that money. But then imagine how they must have felt about having had a treasure on their hands all that time and not even knowing it. In 1991, that artwork, titled *Still Life with Flowers*, sold at an auction for $1.4 million!

A similar thing happened in Old Lyme, Connecticut, where a painting of Niagara Falls had hung for some sixty years in Eno Memorial Hall. In 1991—this must have been a very good year for discovering hidden masterpieces—the owner of a local art gallery spotted the painting hanging over a copy machine. He recognized it as the work of John Frederick Kensett. The original oil, painted in 1855, was appraised at a value of just under $1 million!

There was power and value in the names of those artists, but that power and value had not been appropriated. Just think, if the names of Van Gogh and Kensett are valuable, how much more valuable is the name of the living God, the name which he has agreed to give to you because he loves you so very much!

If you've ever lived in California, you know that people in this state tend to be very fashion-conscious. I've had occasion to browse in some of the stores on Rodeo Drive in Beverly

> *Remember,*
> *you can have God's name*
> *attached to you.*

Hills. Where else can you find a small pocketbook on sale for $600 and a shirt or a blouse for even more? Why are they so expensive? Because of the names attached to them. Admittedly in such cases, it's not the names alone but the fact that the names stand for quality, good workmanship, and status.

It's also not only in places like Beverly Hills that you find name consciousness. People everywhere want to wear Gucci ties or Bill Blass coats or dresses that bear the name of Liz Claiborne or Anne Klein. We've all heard of kids in the inner city who have to wear the right shoes, the ones advertised by Michael Jordan or Shaquille O'Neil. Sometimes it seems that the *only* thing that makes one article of clothing more expensive or more highly regarded than another is the name that's attached to it. I'm not saying that this is right or wrong; it's just the way it is. There is value attached to the right name. Remember, you can have God's name attached to you.

Blessings That Flow from Generation to Generation

There is great benefit in knowing God and in being part of his family—wearing his name—and these benefits are passed down the line from generation to generation to generation. The truth is that it doesn't really matter what your background may be. You can step out of your heritage of disappointment and shame and step into God's family, where he says, Here, I give you my name to wear, and where he promises that his blessings will be handed down from one generation to the next. You can count on the fact that the blessings of God will continue to be given to those people who know him and grow in their relationship to him as well as in obedience to his laws.

I see so clearly the blessings of God in my own life. My great-uncle blessed my father, and my father became a minister. My dad prayed for me, and I became a minister. I know that I'm walking the way God wants me to go, and I have confidence that when my children grow up, they too will walk in God's blessings. I'm not saying they will be ministers, but I am convinced that they will be close to God, whatever it is they choose to do with their lives, and that he will bless them.

You can be the one to start the ball rolling in your own family. You can see to it that the blessings of God are given to your children and your grandchildren. In order to do this, though, you have to teach your children about God and instruct them in his laws. You must bring them into his presence so he can give them his name.

Appropriating the Name of God

The very best way to teach your children how to live for God is through your own example.

How do you obtain the blessing of taking God's name for your own? First of all, you ask him to accept you into his family, cleanse you of your past mistakes, and help you to live a life that is pleasing to him. Then you begin to move out in service to others as his representative.

There is an old hymn that reminds us that God has no hands but our hands. Jesus said that anyone who gives even a cup of cold water in his name will be rewarded. Ask God to help you find ways in which you can be a representative of his love and compassion. All you have to do is open your eyes and look for them; they are all around you.

I saw a poster hanging on someone's wall the other day that said, "Practice random acts of senseless kindness and beauty."

The Bible tells us that when Christ was here in the flesh, "he went around doing good" (Acts 10:38). Here's your example: Go around doing good, and you are using God's name wisely. Practice those random acts of kindness.

Merciful, Just Like Your Father

Physically, we all resemble our parents in some way or other. As a child grows, the similarities often become even more pronounced. A little girl has the same endearing smile as her mother. A little boy uses his hands when he talks, just like his father does. Sometimes the similarities are genetic, as in the case of the smile or the hands, but sometimes the similarities are learned behaviors. For example, a little girl wants a toy vacuum cleaner so she can help her mommy while a little boy wants a tool set so he can work right alongside daddy in his shop. My point is simply that all children learn by watching their parents and by copying the behaviors they see. In this way, if you are a child of God, you should learn by emulating your heavenly Father's behavior.

There are a number of verses throughout the Bible that allude to God's mercy. Luke 6:36 says, "Be merciful, just as your Father is merciful." In Joel 2:13, we find "the LORD your God . . . is gracious and compassionate, slow to anger and abounding in love." Psalm 116:5–6 reads, "The LORD is gracious and righteous; our God is full of compassion. The LORD protects the simplehearted; when I was in great need, he saved me." Jeremiah 33:11 tells us to "give thanks to the LORD Almighty, for the LORD is good; his love endures forever." And in his Sermon on the Mount, Jesus said, "Blessed are the merciful, for they will be shown mercy" (Matt. 5:7).

What does it mean to show mercy? Psalm 41:1 says, "Blessed is he who has regard for the weak." The Hebrew word here, translated as "has regard for," is *hitel*. This can also be translated as "pays attention to." In other words, this passage could be rendered, Blessed is he who pays attention to the weak.

From this, I draw the conclusion that God wants his children to be willing to listen to others. He wants us to open our ears and our hearts to the poor and downtrodden and not to turn away from them simply because they aren't important. One of the best things we can do to help individuals who are going through difficult times is to sit down and listen to them, to be willing to share the burdens that are weighing them down.

A few weeks ago, I was watching a television news story about a woman who was suing her doctor because he had given her a mastectomy when, in fact, she did not have cancer. In the course of the interview she said, "I was on the witness stand. It was a very humiliating experience. The lawyer would interrupt me time and time again, and I never had a chance to tell my story." All she wanted was a chance to tell her story and to talk about the pain and anguish that she was feeling, but nobody cared enough to listen.

More and more in our society I see the need for people to tell their stories, to express the pain they have within them, perhaps even to cry on someone's shoulder. One of the best ways we can move forward in the name of the Lord is to be willing to give our ears to listen and our shoulders to cry on.

Just outside of Washington, D.C., is a clinic that takes care of children dying with AIDS. Many of these children have been abandoned by their parents, so they have no one to hold them or give them the sort of personal attention every child craves. The doctors and nurses and other members of the clinic staff do what they can, but there are too many children and too few clinic personnel for the children to be given the kind of attention they really need.

Before news about this clinic got out, those babies who first came into the clinic would scream and cry for attention. After a while, when it became apparent that their cries weren't going to be answered, they would stop and just lie there in silence.

Sometimes the tears would still roll down their faces, but there wouldn't be a single sound coming out of their mouths. They knew nobody was going to listen or respond, and so they just quit trying.

But then, when the news did get out, some compassionate women came to the clinic and began to care for the children. They often picked them up and caressed them and held them. They sat with them and rocked them and loved them. They saw to it that the babies were fed when they were hungry, had their diapers changed when they were wet, and so on. After a while, these little babies began to cry again. They were still sick with AIDS, of course, but in every other respect they were normal children, now able to give and receive love and to be connected to the world around them.

The same thing happened in Romania to the thousands of children placed in orphanages—warehouses really—under the regime of Nikolai Ceucescu. When the Ceucescu government was overthrown and outside observers were allowed into these orphanages for the first time, they discovered dozens of the children just lying there, never crying, never moving, never showing any emotion or any recognition of what was going on around them. When compassionate women and men began to go in and lovingly care for these children, many of them slowly began to heal. Dozens were ultimately adopted by loving families and are doing better today. It's so important to know that someone cares.

People need an opportunity to say, Hey, I'm hurting. I need to tell my story. What do we need most in America today? We need a listening ear, somebody who is going to care and say, It's okay; I love you.

The primary reason for wanting to show compassion and love to others should be because that's the way God wants us to behave. It is also a means of assurance that we will obtain compassion and love when we are hurting.

As the Bible says, what you give you will receive.

What you sow, you will reap.
Sow an action and you will reap a habit.
Sow a habit and you will reap a character.
Sow a character and you will reap a destiny.
What you sow, you will reap.

Sow compassion and love, and you will reap compassion and love.

God is compassionate. He is always ready to listen. It doesn't matter what it is, if it's on your heart, he wants you to talk to him about it. It may be something that's very small when compared with everything else that's going on in the world today, but whatever it is, if it's important to you it's important to God. He is willing to listen and not only willing, in fact, but *anxious* to listen to you.

God is willing to bless you by giving you his name, but when he does, he expects you to use that name in the right way. He wants you to go forth as his ambassador, as his agent of mercy and healing sent to a broken-down, broken-hearted society.

If ever this world needed people who are willing to go forth as ambassadors of God, it needs them today. Sorrow and terror seem to be everywhere, in the form of gang violence, child abuse, homelessness, crime, hunger, poverty, loneliness, despair, suicide, and addictions of various sorts. The list could go on and on. This world is full of frightened, hurting people, who need to know that someone cares, who need to know that we love them and that God loves them, too.

So you see, taking the name of God upon yourself is both a blessing and a challenge. It's a challenge because it involves a great responsibility. But it's a blessing because God empowers you to handle that responsibility and gives you the assurance that you are part of his family, that you will be able to live under the shadow of his love and his protection forever and ever. And that is a very, very nice place to be!

12

You Can Have a Partnership with God

There was a young preacher, fresh out of seminary, who received a call to his first church, a little country congregation where most of the members made their living as farmers. The new pastor decided that one of the first things he needed to do was to get to know the members of his new congregation. He got out the membership rolls and devised a plan to pay a personal visit to each family, beginning with the As and working his way through the Ws. (There weren't any in the church whose last names began with X, Y, or Z.)

As his first order of business, this preacher went to the Anderson's farm, a beautiful little place with a picture-postcard farmhouse, freshly painted barns, and beautifully manicured fields, including acres of stately corn dancing gracefully in the wind.

161

"Mr. Anderson," the pastor began, "you have a beautiful farm here. It's really impressive."

Looking around, the old farmer nodded in agreement. "Yes, Pastor, God and I have done a pretty good job on this place."

"You and God?" the pastor asked in amazement.

"That's right," came the reply. "God and I are partners. I sow and he grows. But you know, he really couldn't have done this without my help."

Well, of course, the pastor was incredulous when he heard this. "Wait a minute! You really think God needs anybody's help?"

"Well, sure," the old farmer answered. "After all, you should have seen this place when God had it all to himself."

This may be an old joke, but there's a lot of truth to it. The Lord may not need our partnership, but he is willing to have us join together with him in a partnership. This is another great way he is blessing us right now. He is holding out his hand, offering us a full partnership in the administration of this planet. He is saying: You make an effort, and I will bless it. You sow the seed, and I will send the rain and the sunshine and cause that seed to grow. You take a step of faith, and I will bless that step with my power and might. You move forward in an act of loving-kindness, and I will tend to that act and see that it bears fruit.

Genesis tells us that when God created man, he placed him in charge of the earth.

God created man in his own image, in the image of God he created him; male and female he created them. God blessed them and said to them, "Be fruitful and increase in number; fill the earth and subdue it. Rule over the fish of the sea and the birds of the air and over every living creature that moves on the ground."

Genesis 1:27–28

And again:

Then God blessed Noah and his sons, saying to them, "Be fruitful and increase in number and fill the earth. The fear and dread of you

> *Nothing*
> *is going to happen today*
> *that you and God together*
> *can't handle.*
> *(And not only today,*
> *but tomorrow*
> *and the day after tomorrow*
> *and the day after the day after*
> *tomorrow!)*

will fall upon all the beasts of the earth and all the birds of the air, upon every creature that moves along the ground, and upon all the fish of the sea; they are given into your hands. . . . I now give you everything."

Genesis 9:1–3

One way of looking at things is that God is the owner of everything, but he has appointed us, his creatures, as his managers. In this way, we are his partners. And, if we are God's partners, we can know that the old saying is true. Nothing is going to happen today that you and God together can't handle. (And not only today, but tomorrow and the day after tomorrow and the day after the day after tomorrow!)

You don't have to live in fear. You don't have to give in to anxiety and stress. If God is your partner, things are going to work out.

God not only invites you to be his partner and share his blessings, he also invites you into a partnership to bring his blessings upon the poor and the brokenhearted. He invites your participation in his plan to transform emptiness and desolation into fullness and joy.

The thirty-fifth chapter of the Old Testament Book of Isaiah offers a list of things the Lord has promised to do for those who serve him:

> The desert and the parched land will be glad;
>   the wilderness will rejoice and blossom.
> Like the crocus, it will burst into bloom;
>   it will rejoice greatly and shout for joy.
> The glory of Lebanon will be given to it,
>   the splendor of Carmel and Sharon;
> they will see the glory of the Lord,
>   the splendor of our God.
>
> Strengthen the feeble hands,
>   steady the knees that give way;
> say to those with fearful hearts,
>   "Be strong, do not fear;
> your God will come. . . ."
>
> Then will the eyes of the blind be opened
>   and the ears of the deaf unstopped.
> Then will the lame leap like a deer,
>   and the mute tongue shout for joy.
> Water will gush forth in the wilderness
>   and streams in the desert.
> The burning sand will become a pool,
>   the thirsty ground bubbling springs.
>   Isaiah 35:1–7

When I read these words from the prophet Isaiah, I start wondering how many people's lives today are little more than deserts? Whose souls are dry and parched? How many people are desperate for the showers of blessings the Lord can give them? They are all around us. And God asks us to become his partners in bringing them to him so he can bless them. First, he reaches down and blesses us, and then he asks us to reach out to bless others.

As an example, I think of a man who once served time on death row in the Mississippi State Penitentiary after being convicted of involvement in Ku Klux Klan bombings during the 1960s. Today, that same man is the associate pastor of a metropolitan church. His name is Thomas Tarrants.

After serving several months of his sentence, Tarrants escaped from prison with two other men. Their escape was short-lived, however, because the FBI tracked them down, surrounded their hiding place, and killed one of them in the gun battle that followed. Tarrants was captured and returned to prison, where he was placed on death row as an extra precaution against further trouble.

It was there that Tarrants began studying the great philosophers. This study of philosophy led him in turn to the Bible. To summarize what happened to Tarrants, the hand of God reached down and touched him while he sat hopelessly in his dark, tiny, grimy cell. When this happened, Tarrants was transformed. The bitterness, anger, and hatred that had consumed him for so long was gone. In its place was the love and peace of God.

Naturally, it was difficult for Tarrants to convince anyone that he had changed. Those who had known him for some time were certain that it was a scam. Others laughed and talked about how common it was for people to "find God" when they were inside the prison only to "lose him" again as soon as they were outside those walls. As time went on, it became more and more apparent that the change in Tarrants's life was real. Even some of his worst enemies came forward to ask the governor of Mississippi for his release.

Eventually, Tarrants was given his freedom (even though this was unheard of in a case involving such a serious crime). He has spent the rest of his life seeking to bless others as God blessed him. Not only is he serving as associate pastor of an interracial church, but he has started a program that trains ministers to go into inner-city areas to help bring positive change in the name of Christ. Tom Tarrants was a recipient of God's great blessings, and he couldn't help but want to bless others.

And he's certainly not alone. If you go into the inner city of most large metropolitan areas, you will find at least one clear example of God's love. Right in the middle of the crime, the poverty, the drugs, and the homelessness, you will find a Christian mission run by men and women who have devoted their lives to helping the poor. In the majority of cases, these missions are run by those who used to be out on the streets, too. Somehow these people were rescued by the love of God. Like Tom Tarrants they now want to spend the rest of their lives bringing the blessings of God to those who are in the same miserable condition they once knew.

That's the way it is. Those who know they have been blessed by God want to bless others. Those who have their eyes open know that they have been blessed by God. They understand that he is blessing them now.

Blessings through a Partnership with Others

God offers to bless you through a partnership with him and also through a partnership with your fellow human beings.

There is an old parable about a man who was approached by a stranger. The stranger explained that he was new in town and asked, "What kind of people can I expect to find here?"

"Well," said the man, "what kind of people lived in your hometown?"

"Oh," replied the stranger, "they were the worst. That town was full of cheaters, liars, and thieves. There wasn't a good person among them."

The man shook his head sadly. "I'm afraid," he said, "that the people here are much the same."

A few minutes after the first stranger went on his way, another one came along. He, too, explained to the man that he was new in town. Again, this second stranger asked what sort of people he could expect to find there.

The man replied, "What kind of people lived in the town you came from?"

"Oh," said the stranger, "they were the salt of the earth. You couldn't ask for better people. Always ready to do anything to help you when you needed it. The finest bunch of people you've ever met."

The man smiled and said, "That's exactly the way I would describe the people who live here."

After the second stranger left, a woman who had overheard both conversations came up to the man. "I don't understand it," she said. "How could you tell one man that the people in this town are terrible and then turn around and tell another that they are among the best people anywhere?"

"Because," the man replied, "you will generally get from people what you expect from them. If someone treats people as if he expects them to be cheaters and liars, they will be. But if someone treats people as if he expects them to be kind and helpful, then that's what he'll get from them."

Treat others the way you want them to treat you, and they *will* treat you the way you want. God gave you two good hands. He expects you to use one of them to reach out and take hold of his hand in partnership, and the other to reach out and take hold of your neighbor's, in partnership. God is blessing you right now by placing into your life people who have the capacity to bless you with their friendship and their love.

Gaining an Understanding of the Blessings of God

We've almost come to the end of our time together. I hope that this book has helped you understand clearly that God is blessing you *right now*, this very moment!

We have discovered that:

- God is blessing you right now.
- God gives everlasting blessings.
- God is blessing you even when life hurts.
- He blesses you by offering you his peace.
- He blesses you with forgiveness.
- God blesses you when you reach out to others.
- He is blessing you by offering you refuge.
- God blesses you with the joy of his presence.
- God is blessing you with his instruction.
- He is blessing you with his name.

God really does desire to bless you. As he says in Jeremiah 29:11, "For I know the plans I have for you . . . plans to prosper you and not to harm you, plans to give you hope and a future." The Lord wants only the best for you. His desire is to bless and prosper you and, because you know this is true, you can face the future with total confidence.

I urge you to look around at some of the blessings God gives us on an almost daily basis.

- sunsets
- rainbows
- flowers
- colors
- things that smell good
- music
- things that taste good
- laughter
- things that are pleasing to the eye
- clouds
- trees
- sunshine
- moonlight
- things that are pleasing to the touch

What happens to good people when bad things happen to them? They see the blessings of God and become better people!

I could continue but I won't. I'm sure you can think of many other ways God blesses us every day. The blessings of God really do go on and on and on.

Occasionally I run into people who tell me they wish they lived in "the good old days" when things were so much better than today. You know what? You and I are blessed to be living right now!

How can I say this? Because we are fortunate enough to live in a time when medical advances have all but wiped out diseases that were rampaging through the world only forty or fifty years ago. We live in a world of advancing technology, where it is possible to communicate almost instantaneously with another person anywhere in the world. We can fly from New York to Los Angeles in less than five hours. Our homes are filled with electronic wizardry such as personal computers and VCRs; never before has so much entertainment been available to so many at such a low price. And, in many ways we are blessed simply because we live in these closing years of the twentieth century.

I am not saying that we live in a perfect country or a perfect world. We have plenty of problems here. But all too often we focus on the negatives and forget about the good and positive things God is giving us, and God is giving us many good things.

Truly, he is blessing you right now. Open up your hands and receive. God loves you far more than it's possible for you to comprehend and, because he loves you so much, you have nothing at all to fear. Not now. Not tomorrow. Not ever.

Heavenly Father, thank you for blessing us the way you do. Help us open our eyes and see all the ways you are blessing us. Help us to take hold of the blessings you want to give us. And help us, in turn, to reach out and bless others. Guide us, guard us, and direct us as we seek to live for you. Help us always to be aware of your presence as we go through life. Amen.

God *is* blessing you right now!